EMPATH & ENNEAGRAM

THE MADE EASY SURVIVAL GUIDE FOR HEALING
HIGHLY SENSITIVE PEOPLE - FOR EMPATHY
BEGINNERS AND THE AWAKENED (2 IN 1)

SARAH HOWARD

CONTENTS

BOOK ONE

*H*ighly Sensitive Person:

A complete Survival Guide to Relieve Anxiety, Stop Emotional Overload & Eliminate Negative Energy, for Empaths & Introverts

INTRODUCTION

"You're too sensitive!" they say. *"You just need to grow a thicker skin."* You hear from well-meaning friends and family. If this sound familiar and you find yourself struggling with self-acceptance and feelings of shame, you could be what's known as a Highly Sensitive Person (HSP) – otherwise known as an Empath.

As someone who bears this gift herself, the author, Sarah Howard has struggled with the ups and downs of feeling like she was at the mercy of other's emotions. On a cold December morning in 2014, while everyone (including Sarah herself) where in good spirits about the up-coming holidays, Sarah was rushing from shop to shop to buy the last minute gifts for her loved ones.

All was well until, whilst waiting in line, she heard someone behind her mutter "people that cut the line make me sick.". Sarah didn't take much notice as she knew she hasn't cut the line and so this lady must be talking about someone else.

"I said," she heard from behind her, "that people who cut in line, make me sick!". This time Sarah felt the outburst might directed at her, so she turned to politely correct this lady who was mistaken.

However, as soon as she turned, the lady started shouting in a confrontational manor, "yeah you! I can't stand the way people think they can do what they like and cut lines like they're the queen of the world!"

"That's not the case!" Sarah wanted to say. "I've been here the whole time! I've never cut a line!", but she couldn't get her words out. She was so shocked and scared by this woman's anger she was left unable to speak.

As the woman continued to berate her, Sarah found herself overcome with anger and fear and sadness. She didn't know what to do and found herself starting to cry. She dropped the gifts she was holding and ran out of the store, distraught.

Throughout the following days she found herself continuing to feel upset, and no matter what she did, or how her friends and family tried to help, she couldn't shake that sadness this any woman at the store has passed on to her.

This ended up ruining her Christmas day, as she was still tense, angry and sad from the experience. This only served to compound her misery and, after waking up on the 26th of December 2014, she decided – *enough was enough!* She was going to figure out *WHY* other people's negative emotions seemed to affect her so powerfully and *HOW* to regain control of her own emotions, energy and life – *once and for all.*

This decision lead her down the path of understanding what affected her and others like her in her. After years of self-experimenting, connecting directly with others and just plain hard work, Sarah has found what she feels to be the most effective and powerful tools to help other Highly Sensitive People forgive their perceived shortcomings and achieve their full self-actualization.

Now, maybe for you someone shouting at you for cutting the line might not elicit the same response. Sarah is definitely on the more-sensitive end of the spectrum of Empaths. But whatever it is you're struggling with in your day to day life, by better understanding your own and other's emotions and energies, you will be better equipped to tackle the world and it's inevitable problems.

This book is the culmination of this years of hard work and research and aims to help teach you the tools and techniques needed to develop resiliency in yourself.

Here's what to expect as you work your way through this book:

In Chapter 1: The Way of The Empath, we'll discuss the history of the term "Empath" and what it means to be an Empath in today's world. We'll walk you through what a typical day looks like for an Empath in the hopes that you can connect and relate to these experiences.

We'll talk about the daily struggles of Empaths, and also the positives of this gift, and how you can start to reframe the beliefs you might have held about being a Highly Sensitive Person.

In Chapter 2: Empath Signs, we'll cover the 29 signs of Empaths so you can see how many you relate two.

This points are a great starting point for people just discovering their gift and should give you many "ah-ha!" moments as you realise there are others like you!

We'll further explore the positive and negative experiences of Empaths, details the specifics of how each aspect affects people's inner and outer lives.

For Chapter 3: The Empath Phenomenon, we'll delve into the research and science of the experience of being a Highly Sensitive Person. Amongst other points, we'll discuss the role that EMFs (Electro Magnetic Fields), Mirror Neurons and Dopamine plays in the life of an Empath.

By understanding the physical realities underpinning this experience, you can apply your gift in even more powerful and impactful ways.

In Chapter 4: Energy Healing Practices, we'll discuss the various methods that you can use to begin to heal your energies with. We'll cover some of the better known practices, like Yoga and meditation, but also some of the lesser-known (and very effective) methods, such as Chakra clearing and Crystal healing.

In this chapter, you'll be given the practical tools to start your healing journey, with guidance at every step on how to fully utilize each practice for the most benefit.

In Chapter 5: Learning To Control Your Energy, we'll discuss the steps you'll need to take to fully identify your own and other's energies. Once you have a solid grasp on the full power that other people's energies can have on you (both positively and negatively), you'll be more effective in controlling your own and other's energies.

For Chapter 6: Designing Your Healing Dream, we'll go into detail about the importance of your Healing Dream. We'll detail what this will look like for you, and how to design your own for maximum effect. This is a step that some people may call being "a bit out-there", but it's such a profound opportunity to take your healing to the next level, it simply can't be ignored.

Chapter 7: The Healing of Your Past. is all about delving into and discovering the effects your past has played on your current life and mind-set. We'll identify the life-lessons you've accumulated and discuss how these may help (or hinder) you in your everyday life. We'll round off by discussing the importance of, and the techniques to, live your life in the present moment.

Chapter 8: Healing Your Inner Child, will cover... how to go about healing your inner child, of course! This is an extension of the previous chapter where we delve deeper in the specifics of your childhood and how what you experienced helped shape the person you are today.

In Chapter 9: Healing Your Present Self, you'll discover how to take a step back from yourself and look at what areas of your life need to be healed. We'll touch on the importance of your new-found self-awareness as well as taking the final steps in releasing the pain and trauma of your past to live your best life. This chapter culminates in the outline for incorporating regular self-healing into your everyday life.

Chapter 10L Practicing Social Healing will challenge you to take everything you've learnt so far, and put it into action within social situations. This chapter is one of the "heaviest"/"hardest" to read, but, everything you've learnt up to this point has prepared you for life-changing steps in this chapter.

We'll discuss the importance of taking full responsibility for yourself and your relationships, and how this shift from victimhood, to a fully-empowered person will help you to overcoming many of the obstacles you might be facing currently in your life.

We'll close by reminding your that life is all about FUN! You need to take the time and give yourself permission to have fun. These mindset shifts, along with the on-going practice of "Advocating for your-self" will leave you confident you can heal yourself and tackle any challenge life may throw at you!

I would encourage you to work your way through this book at your own pace. Try to fully absorb the message of each chapter before moving on. You'll notice, once you reach the latter chapters focusing on healing, that you might feel you have a lot of action-able steps to take, especially if you still live in the stage of your gift where you can't yet identify and control the energy of those around you.

Taking things slowly and giving yourself the time to take each step ensures that you're not overwhelmed.

So, if you're ready to take the first step in under-standing your gift and healing yourself at the deepest level, it's time to start! Take your time and enjoy yourself!

2

THE WAY OF THE EMPATH

The term Empath has recently become a popular topic within the spiritual community, as people begin to realize that being sensitive is a gift and not something to be derived or ridiculed.

As an Empath, or Highly Sensitive Person (you'll notice we'll use these two terms interchangeably throughout the book), you have a unique gift that allows you to truly feel the needs of others, of the world and the of universe as a whole. This means, you have the unique ability to be a powerful, positive healer of the world. Your gift gives you the opportunity to feel where you can offer more love and compassion and then give this love and compassion as a way to contribute to this loving planet's vibrations.

Unfortunately, in some cases, life as an Empath can lead to obsessive behaviors that deplete your energies and prevent you from experiencing the real wonders of your gift. If you know you're an Empath, or if you suspect you might be, then you likely have many questions about what this gift means and where it comes from.

We'll explore in this chapter what it means to be an Empath, why you live with this gift and how this gift can help you live out the real purpose of your life.

We'll start with the history of what it means to be an Empath and cover the more modern definition to help you build your understanding of your gift and how it fits into the universe's unique makeup.

The History of Empaths

. . .

In recent years, the term Empath or Highly Sensitive Person has emerged throughout many different cultures as a way of describing people who were appear to be in some way emotionally or mystically sensitive to others. Empaths were regarded as gifted healers, philosophers and spiritual teachers in ancient African and First Nations tribes.

These tribes, known to offer their Empaths special blessings and compassionate treatment in exchange for sharing their gifts with the tribes, continue to regard them as such.

Psychologists interested in helping people around the globe understand Empath's unique gifts and how they can master these sensitivities, have recently popularized the phenomena. Dr. Carl Rogers has played an pivotal role in advancing the understanding of Empaths and empathic gifts in recent history by suggesting that this may be a parapsychological phenomenon. In essence, he believes that this is a unique way for certain people to understand and support others in their lives at a deeper level than previously thought possible.

"Sometimes listening to someone else isn't enough,"

Dr. Rogers says, "because empathy from others is what they need - Empaths, who have the highest degree of empathy, are wonderful in offering this unique support to people."

Being an Empath in Today's World

Life as an Empath in today's world is entirely different from how it was in the past for recognized Empaths. Empaths were revered by their societies and were offered constant support, compassion and respect by those around them.

However, seemingly in Western cultures, the inverse was true. People who experienced greater sensitivity than others were considered weak and were often shamed by their peers for their sensitive behaviors. As a result, society became grueling and uncomfortable for Empaths, especially those who had no idea that they were Empaths to begin with.

The understanding of what the term "Empath" means has developed over time, and many

Empaths have been given the opportunity to explore their gifts with a better understanding of their gifts and why they experience what what do.

This also offers a chance to experience a greater sense of compassion for themselves, since they're now able to understand that they're not *at all* weak. In fact, they're incredibly powerful and have the ability to change the world as we know it by offering their loving, compassionate and empathic gifts to the people around them.

As society continues to shift to being more compassionate towards its sensitive beings, Empaths have the opportunity to gain a better understanding of themselves and their community's admiration.

Instead of being ridiculed for their abilities and personality traits, many are finding safe sanctuaries in the world where they can participate in society and play an active role in their lives. The era of being a cursed Empath who was considered weak is quickly coming to an end, as Empaths are now truly beginning to be understood and respected for their amazing gifts.

A Day in an Empath's Life

As an Empath, you might have noticed that your daily life can be very different from the lives of those around you. If you have yet to find a group of people who understand what it feels like, it can feel isolating, uncomfortable or frustrating, when you first try to explain your experiences to others. Your previous lack of the deeper experience of being an Empath means you're not able to fully convey of how powerful you are. Chances are, when you wake up, an immense amount of energy is instantly felt. You can literally "feel" the energy of the day from what day it is, which may or may not play into how you feel throughout the morning.

Your experiences of the morning can also play a significant part on your energy for the day. If they're positive, like being welcomed by your happy dog and having breakfast with your generally positive family, your energies will likely feel whole and nourished. However, if you wake up to a messy home, a spouse that is constantly grumpy in the morning or a sad child who has a nightmare, you can find you start the day with with relatively intense, negative energies that match those of those around you.

This can be challenging if you're consciously trying to face your day with a positive energy, but instead you find yourself feeling overwhelmed and drained before the day even starts. If you work or spend your day with other people, the bulk of your working day can be overwhelming, as you take on these energies constantly and feel them as if they were your own. For example, if someone arrives at work late and everyone is cranky because it's slowed down the workflow, you might feel irritable and exhausted, because you take on both your own, and everyone else's crankiness.

If you're lucky enough to spend your days working in a positive environment, you may find yourself feeling exceptionally positive throughout the day, but you might still feel drained after work because of how many *different* types of energy you encountered throughout the day. Whether your day was positive or not, the amount of energy you experienced around you was probably overwhelming and made you feel like you had nothing left for yourself.

You can spend your evenings laying low and doing nothing as a way to relax and allow your energy to fill up again the next day. If the flow of other's energies resonates with you every day, you experience the life of an Empath who hasn't yet fully understood, accepted and mastered his Empathic gifts.

As we progress through this book, you'll find that your life doesn't have to feel like this at all and that you can experience a more positive and enjoyable life without feeling depleted at the end of each day. In fact, you'll discover how you can generate even more energy for yourself so you can make the most of your life, while still mastering your unique empathic gift!

The Empath Calling

Being especially sensitive to others energies means you were born with an amazing gift that can truly help you change the world. You can be the person that helps to overcome the collective suffering that wars, greed, and ignorance have exerted on humankind for hundreds of years.

You have the gift of being able to fully listen to and understand people. You can support them in their healing journeys using your ability to experience complete empathy to an incredibly deep level. When someone needs love, compassion, guidance or reassurance, they know they can come to you and experience it. Since this is what the world lacks greatly right now, you're the perfect person to offer it to the world. You've probably seen this trend in your life with the number of people who have looked for support or compassion from you. This pattern may have become so regular that you find yourself withdrawing from or avoiding relationships because it can sometimes feel that more energy is needed than you have left.

This can lead to feelings of guilt or loneliness in your life, but it can seem like a reasonable price to pay to avoid feeling overwhelmed by your energy and everyone else around you. Empaths are often called to caring roles, often choosing to work as healers, caretakers, advocates, and teachers. This is because they have the unique characteristics that can make a real difference in the world and people around. However, their Empathic gifts, left unmanaged, can lead them to feel overwhelmed and unable to pursue these vocations for fear of being constantly drained and energy-zapped.

If an Empath is able to learn how to master their gift and use their empathic talents to their advantage, they will find that they can make massive changes in the world around them by pursuing these roles and entering them fully.

It's known that some of our time's most influential leaders, healers and teachers are Empaths. Oprah Winfrey, Deepak Chopra, Princess Diana, the Dalai Lama, and Mahatma Gandhi are all famous Empaths who have taken on their roles, mastered them and fulfilled their life purposes. This proves that it can be done and can be done beautifully as long as you take the time to truly understand yourself, have compassion for yourself and fulfill your own needs as an Empath and as a human being.

. . .

A Realistic Understanding

Once you understand that your purpose in life is to heal the world, it can feel pretty intense or over-whelming. On the one hand, because of your nature and the way you naturally interact with those around you, combined with your innate calling, you might find that it makes sense. On the other hand, it can still seem daunting or even impossible to take on such an enormous task if you don't take the time to visualize it realistically and put it into perspective. I want to remind you that *you're not alone*! Hopefully this helps you feel a little less intimidated by all of this.

You're not the only Empath that exists, and you're not the only Empath that supports the goal of healing those around us. There are thousands, if not, hundreds of thousands of other Empaths out there who are all dedicated to supporting this journey of healing that we're going through collectively at this time. All you have to do is learn how to master your-self and contribute in the way you feel most aligned with. By learning how to master your own energies, you can immediately make positive use of yourself and your purpose to change the world around you. You can do this by being a local energy healer, teacher or philosopher, if you feel like focusing on a more intimate, local-level would fit best with your goals. Or you can do it by carrying out a large-scale mission, like having a public talk show to reach the masses. (think, Oprah).

There are no rules to this and there is nothing that says that one dream or purpose is more or less worthy than another, no matter how big or small it may seem. You must trust that you were born with the divine ability to fulfill your purpose and that your purpose is your calling in life, no matter what anyone says or thinks about it. Some of the Empaths most important vocations came from innovating a new way of contributing their own energy and purpose to the collective and serving them in the way they felt most aligned with.

There's no *right* way to contribute. If you're still not sure what your personal calling is, you're likely to struggle to spend that time with yourself and develop self-awareness because you're constantly being drained by society's energy. Don't worry, when the time is right, your calling will appear and appear to you and all you have to do then is stay on track. Pursue your healing journey and do what you feel is right. It's going to appear before you know it and you'll have the exact blueprint for what you're here to achieve in life.

3

EMPATH SIGNS

*I*f you read the last chapter and felt a deep resonance with what you read, you can feel pretty confident that you're an Empath. However, you might be wondering what your empathic gift entails and what aspects of yourself reflect your gift.

Empathy appears in many ways, so you've likely come across many instances where empathy has affected or changed your life and how you interact with the world around you.

To help you feel comfortable and confident, and to help you understand precisely how being an Empath affects your life, we'll explore the signs of being an Empath and the common symptoms you're likely to have experienced in your life. This will help you determine whether or not you are an Empath, and how empathy affects your life. Although we'll discuss a number of signs in this chapter, it's important to rember that resonating with just one of these is enough. It's not uncommon that Emapths will feel a connection to three or more of then, but don't feel discouraged if only one or two fit your experience of life.

Each Empath is somewhat unique in the way their gift manifests itself. Therefore, you might find that some of these signs resonate more intensely than others. You might also agree to some extent with each of them. As long as you can resonate deeply with at least one or two of these signs, you're likely to be an Empath. You'll probably experience more or experience these signs to a deeper level as you dive into your gift and embrace the reality of Empath.

The Signs of Empaths

People Point Out Your Sensitivity

Other people tend to recognize increased sensitivity in Empaths, which they often point out at different points in their lives. Your increased sensitivity may have been praised in the past as a wonderful sign that you have a big heart, or it may have been used against you in those who claim your sensitivity is a weakness. People who point out your sensitivity are a common experience for many Empaths.

Being sensitive to the point where others recognize that sensitivity can feel like a blessing or a curse depending on how others react it to it. If you have been made to feel intimidated about your sensitivity in the past, you might feel that this is a weakness and that you must try to be stronger and have a harder "shell." In this case, you'll need to focus on healing your inner child from these incidents of intimidation so that you can accept your sensitivity as a gift.

If you've experienced this as a positive thing in your life, like people commenting on how much they value you as a sensitive person, you might sometimes find yourself being exploited for your sensitivity. Although this isn't always the case, many Empaths tend to lean on pleasing people and "give" their energy through their sensitivity to maintain a positive environment around others. If you're around people and you begin to experience the emotions they're experiencing themselves, you're probably an Empath.

Empaths often report that they feel other people's emotions deeply and often express them more clearly and effectively than the other person could. For example, if someone hears some bad news and feels shocked and sad, you might experience the energy from that news through them, and more intensely than them so you may find yourself crying from the news, even though it doesn't affect you. This display can be even more "showy" than the other person who can struggle to feel and process his emotions effectively.

It can also feel overwhelming for you to be around people who don't know how to process their emotions effectively. You might feel a constant, intense feeling inside of people who tend to bottle up their emotions, which comes from having too many unexpressed emotions. You might also feel over-whelmed from people who express themselves loudly or aggressively, because the energy output is so intense.

Negative Feelings Overwhelm

Empaths are often overwhelmed by negative feel-ings. This includes being overwhelmed by other people's negative feelings as well as your own. Nega-tive feelings often come with a heavy, dense energy that can leave an Empath feeling as if the emotion itself is literally weighing them down. As a result, you can be exhausted, frustrated and find it difficult to express yourself. An intense desire to get the energy away from you can lead to negative feelings being avoided or denied as a way to avoid facing this heavy density of emotion.

Something surprising is that many Empaths aren't fully aware that positive feelings can also become overwhelming. Positive energy emits at a high frequency and can lead to anxiety-like feelings, especially when experienced for longer periods. After an intense positive experience, it's not unusual for an Empath to feel particularly drained because the energy frequency was so high and intense. If you're an Empath who hasn't yet learned to master your gift, you'll probably find yourself extremely overwhelmed in crowded areas as a result of this.

Anywhere with a large crowd of people can feel draining, due to the sheer amount of energy you constantly have to absorb and process. You might feel as if you're moving slowly as the energies around you move at the speed of light. The two completely different frequencies can lead to an intense sense of overwhelm and exhaustion soon follows. Due to this, the desire to leave or avoid all crowds is something that grows within many Empaths in an effort to avoid the uncomfortable feelings associated with them. If you feel intense anxiety about crowds but you would prefer to be an outgoing and extroverted person, the internal conflict can be extremely frustrating when you try to balance your anxiety with your extroverted desires.

The good thing is that you can actually change the way you approach crowds and successfully engage in extroverted experiences and even thrive by learning how to master your energy and manage yourself in places with more busy energies.

In a world where everyone seems to strive to reconnect with their intuition, you might struggle to relate to this desire. To you, being in contact with your intuition has always come to you naturally, and you might be surprised that it's not the same for others. You have always experienced input from your intuition as long as you can remember, and it's always been right. However, whether you chose to believe it or not, it can be an entirely different story. Because of how "hard" society has been for so long, many Empaths blatantly ignore their intuition and instead follow what they were "supposed to do." This often leads to the wrong path being drawn and the wrong things being done that can lead to a myriad of problems and consequences.

If you have found yourself struggling to trust your

intuition despite it always seeming correct in the end, you're not alone. As you heal your relationship with yourself and your higher consciousness, your ability to trust in and act on your intuition will increase, and you'll find yourself not struggling nearly as much.

Your Pain Threshold Is Low

Many Empaths find that their actual pain threshold for both physical and emotional experiences is particularly low. Getting your vaccine shots, dealing with a paper cut, or having a headache may feel particularly intense for you. You might have even found it to be so bad that you're embarrassed to experience these things around others for fear of how they may react to your response to a painful stimulus.

You might find yourself avoiding places with a lot of pain, like doctor's offices or hospitals because it's challenging for you to be around so many people who are in pain. Not only do the others in pain create a difficult energy for you to embrace, but also the building's own energy can affect you. You prefer to avoid these places as often as possible so that the energy of pain doesn't need to be embraced.

Your Physical Awareness Is Strong

People probably don't believe you, but you can feel

sick before any symptoms even begin. You might feel that something creates sickness in your body and you can recognize what changes happen in your body, even if these changes aren't significant. You might not even be able to describe them as a particular symptom at times, because it's so subtle and yet so obvious to you. Headaches, gastrointestinal disorders, and muscle pain are likely to be the same. Some people may think that you're a hypochondriac because you constantly reflect on changes in your body and in some cases, you might be worried that something bad is happening.

When you try to explain things to doctors, they may struggle to get a clear diagnosis because what you experience is something that most people don't talk about, so they can't link the symptoms to any recognized disease. Most people probably experience these symptoms, but they don't recognize them because they lack the physical awareness you have. However, your concerns are worthwhile and, in the end, there's often a discovery of something that can cause your symptoms. The main reason they weren't previously considered is that your doctor probably didn't recognize that you noticed them earlier than others would have, so they assumed that the likely causes were unlikely.

You Find Media Or Images That Are Negative Hard To Watch

You probably feel extremely uncomfortable seeing images of cruelty or hearing stories of pain experienced by others. You might feel nauseous and nearly sick by the stories you hear or the pictures you see. You might also feel an intense outbreak of pain almost as if you were also suffering. You have probably created an environment in which you don't pay attention to the news, read tabloids or scroll through certain social media pages because you fear the pain you'll experience if you find a negative article. Instead of risking it, you would prefer to avoid it and keep your energy safe and free from any sickness or pain from such stories or images.

You Can Spot A Liar

You can intuitively tell when someone doesn't tell you the truth. Although you probably can't explain it, you can feel inside whenever someone tells you a lie or someone around you deliberately holds the truth back. It's an energy that makes you feel skeptical and uncomfortable and supports you in your belief that what you said was dishonest. The energy of people who lie can feel extremely uncomfortable for you, so you can completely avoid liars. If someone you know or spend time with is a perpetual liar, you're likely to minimize your time with them, or find a polite way to end your relationship with them. The feeling itself is uncomfortable and can be very draining, and you don't want to spend time with liars. You avoid such relationships like the plague.

Stimulants or medicines seem stronger

If you take a stimulant or medicine, or anything else that might in some way "intoxicate" you, you're likely to be affected much more than the average person. Caffeine, for example, can have a particular impact on you by making you feel excessively ener-gized whenever you ingest it. Alcohol can be some-thing you have to enjoy in moderation to avoid overdoing it, and it can even make your empathetic gifts more overwhelming than normal in some cases. Many Empaths say they even have difficulty taking ibuprofen for headaches because they have such a strong impact on them. Due to your increased phys-ical awareness, you might also find it difficult to accept the differences associated with taking medi-cines like painkillers. Whenever you feel them in your system, a sense of discomfort or anxiety can be created that lasts until the medication leaves your system completely. This can instead lead you to avoid painkillers and lean to natural remedies, which ultimately make you feel better.

Experiencing the symptoms of others

The ability to experience symptoms of other people is a common and sometimes strange symptom that people experience when they're Empathic. If you've ever been around someone who reported having a certain symptom, like having a headache, and then you started to feel a headache, you're an Empath. This particular dynamic can be challenging because others may feel that you try to compete with them and their symptoms as a way to get others' attention. The reality is, it doesn't happen. Instead, you feel so strongly sympathetic to this person that you take on their symptoms. The sympathetic pregnancies experienced by husbands or other people who are particularly close to pregnant women are a common and sometimes humorous case in which this happens. For example, if a husband is with his pregnant wife in the other room and he begins to experience what he feels is contractions, he experiences sympathetic resonance.

Empaths often get this, and sometimes they don't even necessarily know about people. Since Empaths tend to be sympathetic to everyone, they can take these strange symptoms from anyone, sometimes even without the person actually saying anything about the symptom. One unfortunate side effect of being an Empath is that you probably tend to attract narcissistic people into your life. Narcissists are people who have no capacity whatsoever to experience or empathize. Although they can effectively imitate signs of empathy, they can't feel it in themselves, which often leads to harmful and harmful behaviors.

Narcissists tend to be very abusive and manipulative, and their "victims" are known to be causing immense psychological and emotional suffering. As an Empath, you have one thing narcissists lack: empathy. Also, you have an excess compared to others. You're therefore an ideal candidate for them because they know that you're more likely to be empathetic to them and their internal suffering. At some level, you can feel the pain they have experienced, which has led them to be unable to empathize with themselves or anyone around them, and this leads you to feel sorry for them. Even if you can't fix them, you might find yourself trying to fix them. In the end, the narcissist manipulates and hurts you and the cycle never ends. You must learn to put an end to relations with narcissists and remove the belief that you're responsible for their ability to heal themselves if they're not willing or able to heal.

You might benefit from reading more about narcissism and understanding how these relationships are the way they are, and why they never change. This can help you end your relationship with narcissists and prevent you from entering into future relationships so that you can stop being exploited by people who cannot truly understand that they're exploiting you. You tend to be extremely compassionate towards others when they're suffering because you "get" them in a way that no one else can .

As a result, you'll probably find many people coming to support you. You might even find that people you have never met before seem to know you're supportive and Empathetic, so they open themselves up to you without knowing who you are. Of course, you still support them, as they suspected because that's who you are. Supporting others seems to be your natural gift, and sometimes you can even do it to the detriment of yourself.

Your empathy can make it difficult for you to recognize when you need to stop supporting others and instead offer yourself support so that from time to time you can give too much of yourself and energy to others.

You Experience Fatigue

Often the constant absorption and expression of energy in you and around you can lead you to a constant sense of exhaustion. Sometimes the exhaustion may feel purely mental, and you might feel that your physical body can continue for a while.

This type of fatigue can lead to brain fog, concentration difficulty and an inability to engage in your environment. As a result, you can retreat to rest and do nothing, even if you could keep going physically if you wanted to. This doesn't mean you also don't have physical fatigue. In fact, even after a day of doing almost nothing, you might feel completely mentally and physically exhausted. If you're surrounded by too many people, just sitting at a desk can seem physically and mentally exhausting.

Even a basic outing like grocery shopping or clothing shopping can overwhelm you and make you feel like you can't work without a good rest. While other people do things at all hours of the day, you can plan your outings around rest periods so that after all the exhaustion you experience, you can slow down and catch up.

Your Inner Life Is Very Vibrant

Empaths tend to have a very vibrant inner world. You can find yourself rich in visions, dreams, ideas, and hopes that you regularly maintain and cultivate. If you're left to your own devices, these inner experiences are likely to envelop you in spending time dreaming, creating or enjoying more mystical experiences like astral travel or lucid dreaming. Unlike others, you find yourself enriching and enjoyable because of the many things you need to think about, dream and create. In fact, you might find that you're overwhelmed and frustrated if you don't have enough time alone to engage in your inner world.

You regularly schedule a time to be alone and enjoy things by yourself, which helps you feel enriched and lively so that you can enjoy life more vibrantly and with more fulfillment.

You experience sensitivity to sounds and sensations

If you're not careful, sounds and sensations tend to create extremely overwhelming energies in you. As an Empath, you might find that you feel overwhelmed and exhausted by certain sounds or the volume of different sounds. Some sounds and sensations can also stimulate other sensations within you that create a sense of pain or discomfort.

Many people understand that listening to nails on a chalkboard or the jiggling of keys can make their spine shiver. You probably have many triggers for these types of uncomfortable sensations that aren't strictly related to sounds. You might also find that other sounds or sensations create an incredibly good sensation in you. For example, some relaxing soundtracks can almost instantly make you feel a real sense of calm that can easily override any emotion you experienced before.

You can find different sounds and textures in your environment, as well as lights and visual aids to create these positive and pleasant sensations.

You can feel extremely overwhelmed and exhausted by trying to achieve too many different things at once.

Trying to do something as simple as eating and watching a movie, for example, can feel overwhelming. This can be worsened when you try to combine too many different things, like completing a task while holding a conversation and simultaneously trying to write down notes about something. Or, if you go shopping for groceries and try to keep track of your list while navigating a busy aisle and listening to your husband, you might be especially overwhelmed. Often, when you try to do too many things at once, you feel frustrated and irritated by the feelings of overwhelming. You might find that when you multi-task, you may tell someone else something unkind or harsh because you find it difficult to focus and you feel frustrated.

This can lead to feelings of guilt and even more frustration, leading to a strong and challenging spiral of negativity from your multi-task attempt. Since you know that multi-tasking can cause so much frustration, you probably try to avoid it at all costs.

You have to manage your environment.

It's not unusual for an Empath to feel like managing their own environment. Trying to gain a sense of control over your environment by managing everything and everyone who enters it's probably your way to ensure that the energies aren't overwhelming.

If you're in an environment you're struggling to manage, you might feel like you have to leave the environment because you just can't effectively interfere with it. In your home, you're probably pretty particular about not only how things look, but also how they feel. You're probably decorating and organizing in a way that feels good to you, even if it doesn't necessarily make sense for anyone else. Your environment may look confused or disoriented to others, but it looks perfect for you.

You don't enjoy being around selfish people

When you're around someone who acts in a self-centered way, you probably immediately try to leave that interaction. Egoists tend to create feelings of frustration and anxiety in Empaths because they can become energetic vampires that absorb your energy.

This may feel draining, overwhelming and exhausting. If you have a relationship with someone who is selfish and you can't end it, like a relationship with a selfish boss or sibling, you might try to create as much distance as possible in that relationship. You feel as if you can avoid being drained by this person by avoiding them, minimizing the time you spend communicating and trying to buffer your encounters with another person.

You can feel things you don't feel

Others may say it's weird, but you can feel the energy of the things around you. Things that don't even have feelings, like inanimate objects or certain days of the week, can have a very real and strong energy in your mind. For example, if you see a toy on the wrong shelf and a group of the same toys on a different shelf, you might feel obliged to return the strangely placed object to the other group. It can feel sad or lonely for you, so you have to put it back with the rest of your "friends.".

Things like days of the week, seasons, and even specific words all have the energy for you. For example, if you were to wake up on a Sunday, it would have a completely different energy than a Tuesday based on the day itself, regardless of the content of your calendar or the mood of someone around you. You can also feel a sense of joy at certain positive words and a sense of nagging suffering at certain negative words. These energies may not make sense to anyone but you, but you're sure you can feel them, and they have a great impact on you.

Listening is one of your strengths

You're a great listener in any conversation. You can intuitively "hear" everything the person doesn't say above what they say, which leads you to know what they mean or feel, even if they have struggled to communicate effectively. This ability to hear unspoken information means that you can understand people in a way other people don't.

People often feel very well received around you and as if they can express themselves more authentically because they know that you "get it." You can even be actively involved in a career or hobbies that revolve around listening because you're so good at it. It can be fascinating for you to listen to people and hear everything they do and don't say and give them a sense of true understanding. This is especially true if you have the healer's or teacher's Empathetic call. In your rich inner world and your constant energy alertness can often create incredibly wonderful and enriching life experiences. However, in certain circumstances, it could also make you feel extremely bored and withdrawn.

Trying to perform everyday tasks, like listening to board meetings or entering data into computers can be extremely boring for you because your mind wants to be actively involved and work. It's used to being "on the go" so it gets frustrated and tries to find new things to do whenever you're stationary or slowed down. You can regularly lean towards more enriching experiences that draw your natural talents for communication or creation as a way to curb your boredom.

These types of experiences enable you to play more enjoyably with energy and help you feel better in your life. You can feel your energy coming out to play when you engage in these experiences, and the experience probably fulfills your whole sense of being with feelings of joy and satisfaction.

Many Empaths experience an introverted lifestyle because they struggle to engage in active or overwhelming environments. Empaths who are naturally shy or unable to manage their energy more healthily tend to isolate themselves from the excessively energetic external world. Empaths can minimize the amount of energy around them and feel more confident in controlling themselves and their responses to it by retreating into an introverted lifestyle. Even Empaths who want to be extroverted are likely to retreat as a way to save themselves from the world's external energies.

This can lead to feelings of inner conflict and frustration as the Empath struggles to decide whether to go out and get involved in the world and feel overwhelmed or stay at home and take care of their energies.

Intimate relationships may feel overwhelming

For some Empaths, it can be particularly overwhelming to engage in intimate relations. The intimate relationship can feel like an energy pit where Empath needs to invest more of itself than it can comfortably, even if the relationship follows a healthy dynamic. For an Empath who is used to living alone or alone, it can be overwhelming and frustrating to welcome someone new to their space. They can find themselves completely avoiding intimate relationships so that they can control their personal space more effectively.

If you feel that intimate relationships are especially challenging for you, Empaths who aren't yet clear on how to establish and maintain healthy energy boundaries between themselves and others are likely to experience a common setback. As you learn to heal your energies and assert your boundaries, building and nurturing intimate relationships will be much easier for you.

Nature often feels amazing to you

Empaths have amazing experiences in nature. While nature itself is beautiful for anyone who chooses to enjoy time in it, Empaths can enter nature as a way to nurture their sense of well-being and release the energy accumulations they may experience.

Nature is a base for Empaths to go to that helps them finally feel free to be as they should be. If you find that nature itself is like a friend who helps you to live your best life, it's likely that nature is where you finally have the opportunity to feel peaceful in your life. Spending plenty of time in nature can help you feel nurtured and healed so that you can fully enjoy your life. You can also bring nature indoors with house plants and animals that can help you feel connected to nature's beauty without spending all your time outdoors.

You've got a big heart

You're probably a loving and kind person. Empaths are known for their great hearts and their ability to show love without reserve or inhibition to many different people. Empaths rarely feel that love must be "earned" or given in any slow way.

They're glad to share their love and kindness with anyone with whom they can cross paths and do so with their own heart's generosity. Empaths don't distribute large amounts of love because they expect to be loved back, but because the energy of love fulfills an Empath and they love to share it with everyone. If you find yourself dropping love notes here and there and the heart emoji is one of your most used emojis, you're likely to be an Empath. Your desire to spread love everywhere comes from your inner divine purpose of love and compassion to heal the collective. The more you share your love with those around you, the better you'll feel.

Your Search for Truth

Empaths strongly dislike the energy of lies and dishonesty, so much so that they often find themselves searching for the truth in life. They like to surround themselves with honest people who also pursue the truth, as their energy tends to feel more "pure" and "clean". Empaths can easily detect the dishonesty they're taught in the media, politics and even in education. They rarely fall into society's traps and almost always seek ways to embody and embrace collective truth and personal truth in their own lives.

If you're skeptical about what the collective tends to regard as "true" and regularly seek ways to understand what the real truth is, you're likely to be an Empath who seeks honesty. By finding honesty, Empaths can support society by healing, teaching and advocating the truth and ending many of the various sufferings faced by society. We're constantly moving towards a new, healthier society thanks to Empaths.

You experience frequent swings in mood

You can experience frequent mood swings as an Empath who isn't actively aware of how they can manage their own energy field in any different situation. Mood swings arise as a result of the people around you sapping your energy. This is just like experiencing the symptoms of other people, except that you also have emotions. You might find this symptom increased in larger crowds or in particularly emotional environments.

This is because many more people are surrounded by emotions that affect your energy. In quiet and calm environments, though, it can still happen. Even simple weather changes, the hour on the clock, or the energy of your environment (or social media news feeds) can affect your energy, which then affects your mood.

Beating around the Bush

Empaths don't commonly beat around the bush. They realize that holding the truth back or trying to tell it in a nicer way can defeat the message's purpose and prevent the other person from fully understanding it. Even if it's hard and uncomfortable, it's almost always said by an Empath.

4

THE EMPATH PHENOMENON

*T*he phenomenon of empathy is a way for psychologists and psychiatrists to look into the world of Empathic gifts and discover why all Empaths feel, think and act in the same way. Researchers have discovered five main reasons why Empaths are this way by looking into the minds of Empaths. They found out how the mirror neuron system, electromagnetic fields, emotional infection, increased sensitivity to dopamine and synesthesia all come together to support Empaths with their gifts.

There's a science behind your gifts that explains why they work and how they affect you. We'll explore these five factors in this chapter and discover how they help you to be an Empath. This will help you to feel more confident about your gift by realizing that it's very normal and experienced by many people. By understanding the science of Empaths, we can also discover how healing can take place so that you can heal yourself and experience life as a strong Empath that thrives every day. You don't have to feel like you're suffering from your sensitivity – *you can embrace it.*

The Mirror Neuron System

There's a specific group of specialized brain cells in your brain designed only for compassion purposes. These brain cells work in a way that allows people to reflect other people's emotions or feelings, like fear or joy. We can experience compassion for each other with these brain cells so that we can support each other in many different ways throughout life. For example, if your child cried, your mirror neuron system would also make you feel sad. If your friend was happy with their recent promotion at work, you'd be happy *for* them, as well as *with* them. Through this ability to reflect the emotions of others, you can truly share your experience and offer your support in any way.

This helps us to deepen our emotional relationships and helps us to have a stronger sense of community with those around us. Empaths are thought to have a set of hyper-responsive mirror neuron cells that allow Empaths to resonate with those around them at an even deeper level. This allows Empaths to feel even deeper links with those around them, allowing them to feel as if they can feel another person's emotions or pain. Since the resonance is deeper and the mirroring is stronger, Empaths can even cry with someone who is in pain because they can so strongly reflect the emotions of the other person.

Narcissists, sociopaths, and psychopaths are in contrast to Empaths. These are people who are thought to have what is known as an "empathy deficient disorder", which means that their mirror neuron system is in fact underactive. These people are unable to experience unconditional love and tend to harm others as a way of feeling good in their own lives. They're known to cling to Empaths or people who probably experience higher levels of Empath because they long for Empath themselves, but can not produce Empathic emotions on their own.

Electromagnetic Fields

Science has shown that both the heart and the brain are actively able to produce electromagnetic fields pulsed into the individual's space. The HeartMath

Institute claims that these electromagnetic fields are capable of transmitting information to other people about the energy of a person, like their emotions (energy in motion). In general, everyone can sense and collect information from these electromagnetic fields intuitively, even if they don't realize that they're actively doing so.

Empaths are believed, however, to be more sensitive to these energy fields and can often be overwhelmed by them because they don't know what is happening and may not be able to tell the difference between their own electromagnetic field and that of someone else's. With their own electromagnetic fields, we can intuitively pick up the moon, the sun, the earth, and many other things.

Empaths are also thought to be more in tune with these electromagnetic fields, as with other humans. Most Empaths believe without a fraction of a doubt that the electromagnetic output of the sun, moon, and earth can significantly influence their energy and mind. That said, not everyone realizes that it's from the electromagnetic field supported by science that exists around different people and things.

Emotional Contagion

It's believed that a phenomenon known as "emotional contagion" is part of an Empathic ability to feel so strongly that other people too. Research has shown that the average person can sense and understand other people's emotions when they're nearby. In a household where one person comes home grumpy after a bad day, and then everyone else seems to feel grumpy, emotional contagion can best be recognized.

People can usually "catch" the feelings of someone else and spread over a group of people like a wave, quickly bringing many people into the same emotional experience. Psychologists believe that emotional infection is how groups of people can maintain great relationships: They can understand each other intimately and express similar emotions and connection. As you might have expected, Empaths are believed to have a greater ability to "catch" the feelings of other people through this very phenomenon. As such, they feel the emotions of other people in a particularly intense way that can feel as if the emotion is authentically their own when it actually came from another person.

Increased Sensitivity to Dopamine

Dopamine is a neurotransmitter known to increase brain neuron activity. Responses including pleasure are associated with dopamine. Research has shown that Empaths identified as introverts are known to have a higher dopamine sensitivity than extroverts. What this means is that a shy Empath requires less dopamine to respond to stimuli in their environment with pleasure. This probably explains why introverted Empaths are happier to do something quiet and relaxed than something outgoing: Too much stimulation that produces too much dopamine can lead to feelings of overwhelm and anxiety from significantly increased pleasure.

Empaths that identify themselves as extroverted are still particularly sensitive to dopamine, but the way they process dopamine is entirely different from introverted Empaths. Instead of feeling overwhelmed by excessive dopamine, extroverted empaths actually crave dopamine and find themselves doing things in search of an "increased dopamine high." This means that they regularly engage in active environments, join crowds and enjoy the outgoing side of life as a way of feeling encouraged and positive in their lives.

Synesthesia

A state known as "mirror-touch synesthesia" appears to be most aligned with the phenomenon of empathy. Synesthesia is a neurological condition known to combine two completely different senses in the brain. For example, if you hear a particular piece of music and start to see certain colors in the eye of your mind, synesthesia occurs. Mirror-touch synesthesia is an amplified variation of this condition in which people can actually feel other people's emotions and sensations in their own body.

The way they feel these sensations seem to happen to them when they're not in reality. An Empath would probably not know the difference, however, as they may not know what is actually happening. It may feel so compelling to them that they genuinely believe that something is happening directly to them affects their emotions.

This phenomenon not only explains precisely what happens to Empaths during their empathic experiences, but also gives a clear reason why these things happen. As you now know, being an Empath is a very real experience and is mainly involved in electromagnetic fields and synesthesia with mirror-touch.

The question now is: How can you incorporate healing into your life so you can gain more control over these experiences and stop feeling like you're trapped in a vicious cycle you can't escape?

The answer is rather simple: You have to start healing. One way to begin healing is through energy healing that helps you keep your own electromagnetic fields clear and comfortable. You must also focus on living your own life and taking back any control you might have lost through previous traumatic or painful experiences. You can take control of your energies and start living your best life by healing from your past and allowing yourself to regain control.

5

ENERGY HEALING PRACTICES

*E*nergy healing is one of the most essential healing practices an Empath can learn about. Energy healing practices allow Empaths to immediately begin the healing process without engaging in past, present or future psychological healing. Although these types of psychological healing are still beneficial and often necessary, you can begin to experience significant relief from your symptoms by engaging in energetic healing practices.

There are two ways you can choose to go when it comes to energetic healing practices that give you great support and benefits. One includes having a trained practitioner perform your healing for you, and the other includes working with yourself.

You should ideally engage in both styles to gain

maximum benefits from healing. During times when you want to practice extra self-care or experience a more hands-off approach, an energy healer should be expertly trained in any modality that feels fit for you. Knowing how to heal your own energy allows you to stay in control of your energy and maintain an optimal state of energy health for periods between your sessions.

We'll explore the many varieties of energy healing available in this chapter and how you can use them in your own life. Many of these energy healing practices can be done by yourself or with an experienced practitioner's support so that you can benefit fully from your energy healing experience. If you have never experienced energy healing before, these practices can still be used to start taking control of your energy right now!

Acupuncture

Acupuncture is a type of energy healing that must be carried out in a very specific way by experienced practitioners. Small needles are inserted into your skin at different meridians around the body with acupuncture. Meridians are areas where it's thought that energy builds up and is sometimes "stuck" in the body. It's believed that balance can be restored within the body by gently tapping the needles into these meridians. This healing method is based on ancient Chinese medicine practices designed to help people release chronic pain and emotional and spiritual pain.

This modality of energy works with the psychosomatic system to support complete energetic healing in anyone experiencing it. Acupuncture can be done by a professionally trained therapist who can use acupuncture to take into account your energy healing needs and promote energy flow in your body.

Chakra Clearing

Chakra is a Sanskrit word for "wheel" or "disk" that refers to seven energy centers in the human body. These energy centers are located at the base of your spine, slightly below your belly button, in your solar plexus, in your heart, in your throat, slightly above and between your eyebrows, and at your head's crown.

Each person has their own color, name, and meaning for what these represent in your body, life and spiritual self. Empaths that regularly don't actively clear their energy tend to find their chakras either overactive or underactive. It's believed that unbalance in chakras produces an unhealthy balance within the individual in either state that can lead to negative or unwanted energy experiences.

For example, an overactive third-eye chakra (the one slightly above your eyebrows) can lead to excessive vision or mental stimulation. An inactive third-eye chakra can make you struggle to experience any vision, perhaps even find yourself unable to use your imagination or to engage in creative thinking. Knowing how to clear your chakras begins by finding and feeling them.

A great way to do this is to lie on your back, relax in a meditative state and hover your hand over your body about six inches. Begin by hovering over your root chakra and see if you can feel any energy coming from it. When you "read" each of your seven chakras, move your hand up your body.

Getting a feel for what your chakras feel like is an excellent opportunity to explore and understand your chakras and how they feel to you. You can start practicing chakra clearing with each of your chakras once you have located your chakras. Each chakra typically requires its own unique balancing practice if you don't use Reiki, which addresses each chakra in one holistic process. Each chakra can be balanced on the basis of which your body scan is overactive or underactive. Listed below is each chakra, with its correct name, color, meaning and healing practice defined:

Root Chakra (Muladhara)

Located at the base of the spine, his chakra is red and represents your connection to the earth and the lower body (i.e., legs, knees and feet). By walking barefoot in nature, spending time in nature or eating healthy red foods like tomatoes, berries, and apples, you can heal your root chakra.

Sacred Chakra (Swadhisthana)

Positioned slightly below the belly button, this chakra is color orange and represents your creativity and reproductive organs. You can heal your sacral chakra by swimming, relaxing or eating orange foods like carrots, melons, mangoes or oranges.

Solar Plexus Chakra (Manipura)

Located above the solar plexus, this chakra is yellow in color and represents your personal power and your true essence. The chakra of the solar plexus affects the digestive system. Your solar plexus chakra can be healed by spending time in the bright sun, enjoying a friendly fire or eating yellow foods like bananas, pineapple, turmeric or corn.

Chakra of the heart (Anahata)

This Chakra can be found just above your heart and is green in color. Your emotions are represented here and It affects the heart system and all blood flow-related organs. By breathing in fresh air or spending time with open windows, you can heal your heart chakra. You can also cure it by eating chlorophyll-rich foods like avocado, broccoli, and all leafy greens.

Throat Chakra in your throat (Vishuddha).

This chakra is color blue and represents your ability to speak to others kindly and clearly. Your throat, mouth and oral health are affected. By singing, sitting under a bright blue sky or eating blue foods like blueberries, dragon fruits or currants, you can heal your throat chakra.

Third Eye Chakra (Ajna)

Found between your eyebrows and slightly above them, this chakra is indigo and represents your ability to experience the spiritual world with visions, imaginative thinking and "seeing." Your brain and eyes are affected. By sitting in the sun or eating indigo foods like grapes and blackberries, you can clear your third eye chakra.

Crown Chakra (Sahasrara)

Located on your head and slightly above your head, this chakra is purple and represents your ability to remain connected to the source. It also affects your brain, body, and aura of energy. By connecting with all elements including earth, water, air, and fire, you can heal your crown chakra. The crown chakra is strongly connected to the spirit so that it's not associated with specific food sources.

Crystal Healing

Crystals are a great way to help you experience a healing, nourished body of energy. During certain sessions, like meditation, you can use crystal healing, or you can use crystal healing by carrying a crystal with you during your daily activities. Crystals and gems can help your body, mind, and spirit feel their best when it comes to energy.

Crystals can be used to remove impurities from your energy body, balance energies in the body or inspire and promote specific energies in your body. When it comes to an official healing ritual, crystals are often used alongside meditation by placing them on the body in a so-called "crystal grid." This is done by placing crystals on your body at specific points depending on where the energy is most needed.

Individuals have many different crystal varieties

available, so the best way to ensure that you use the right crystals is to consider your energy needs (i.e., more loving energy) and to select the appropriate crystal for this healing purpose (i.e., rose quartz). You can then lay your crystals on the areas of your body where you want to send or remove this particular energy.

For example, you could place a piece of amethyst over your third eye if you wanted to protect your third eye. If you want a complete crystal healing, the best way to ensure that the right crystals are placed in the right areas to promote your healing is to do one with a crystal healing practitioner. Your practitioner can also help you find ways to use crystal healing at home so you can practice it on yourself.

There are almost endless ways to achieve this when wearing crystals as an opportunity to receive healing from them. Crystals can be worn for your clothes as earrings, necklaces, bracelets, and even hair clips.

Some people also use pocket crystals, which are small flat stones that can be carried in your pocket, and you can rub them all day long between your fingers. It ultimately depends on what you're looking for in your healing to choose the right crystals for your healing practices. There are crystals for virtually every purpose, so the best way to determine which crystals you need is to go to a metaphysical store and ask the store worker to help you find the right crystals. If you're looking for crystals specifically associated with Empathic healing, you should consider including seven great stones in your collection.

Black Tourmaline

Black Tourmaline, an excellent stone to protect your energies and prevent unwanted energies from entering your auric body. If you keep a piece on or with you, any energy that tries to harm you will be pushed away by the energy of the black tourmaline. It's best to wear black tourmaline as a pendant or in your pocket.

Lepidolite

Lepidolite is a great healing stone in the area of Empathic anxiety. You can reduce the anxiety about the energies you feel and experience with lepidolite so that you can approach life more deliberately and with calmer energy. The best way to use lepidolite is to meditate or wear it as a pendant on your heart chakra or third eye chakra.

· · ·

Black Obsidian

Black Obsidian is another excellent stone to protect you against unwanted energy. It's a great way to gain the benefits of black obsidian to carry a piece with you or to keep it in your surroundings. It can be quite sharp, so it's best not to wear or carry this stone in your pocket. If you want to use it during meditation practice, you can also meditate with it near your root chakra.

Malachite

Malachite is an incredible stone for your energy body to deal with emotions and release emotional and energetic blockages. Malachite is excellent for anyone who regularly encounters stressful situations and must be protected from these stressors. Malachite is best worn as a pendant or meditated as it rests on the chakra of your heart.

Hematite

Hematite is known to those who wear it for many

healing benefits. Hematite is an excellent stone for Empaths to help you stay grounded and avoid harmful energies that can try to access your body's energy. You can use hematite to prevent people, like energy vampires, from sucking up your energy. When you meditate, hematite is best stored in your pocket or placed near your root chakra.

Amethyst

Amethyst is an amazing crystal known for its spiritually protective properties. Amethyst can protect you from feeling overwhelmed by energies in your immediate surroundings when used in healing. It can also help to create a sense of calm when you enter more busy environments or environments with stronger or more challenging energies. Amethyst is excellent for Empaths to decide which energies belong to them and to someone else. You can use amethyst in meditation over your third eye, or when you go out to wear almost any form of jewelry.

EFT

. . .

EFT or Emotional Freedom Techniques is an energetic healing practice that an EFT practitioner can practice on themselves. The whole practice is based on tapping on your body with specific energetic meridians and repeating positive affirmations.

The idea is that you lose energy while replacing it with more positive energy that actually helps you live a positive and productive life. EFT can be easily practiced by yourself at any time once you have learned how. However, you need to use specific meridians and tapping patterns to gain maximum EFT value. For this reason, learning how to do it for yourself is the best way to learn how to use EFT for your healing benefit.

Reiki

Originally a gentleman named Mikao Usui founded Reiki. When people engage in Reiki healing, their practitioner can channel universal life energy into them as a way to integrate mind, body, and spirit and encourage natural healing to take place. The Reiki practitioner is therefore not actually responsible for healing but instead encourages the universe to bring healing benefits to that particular person.

When Reiki is practiced, someone who has been tuned by a Reiki instructor to Reiki energy is practicing it. This tuning is considered a necessary initiation to align the practitioner with spirit energy so that they can start their journey to heal others energetically. A tuned practitioner can practice Reiki on himself or on any other consenting person.

This means that if you wanted to, you could heal Reiki as a way to start healing yourself through the Reiki energy. If you don't want to be tuned in the healing of Reiki, you can still receive healings from Reiki practitioners. Many of these practitioners conduct Reiki face-to-face or via remote sessions that can be completed virtually anywhere in the world.

The reason for this is that Reiki practitioners only have to be able to adapt to your energy to direct universal healing energy to your energy. Since true healing comes from the Spirit, you only need to be connected to a source that is an innate gift.

. . .

Quantum Healing

Quantum Healing is similar to Reiki because it uses the energy of life force to carry out the healing practice and support healing in the receiving person's mind, body, and spirit. Although other healings tend to be based on spiritual knowledge and trust, the science of quantum mechanics supports quantum healing.

This healing method considers how quantum energy affects the body and how the energy can be concentrated, amplified and directed to promote certain healing benefits. Those who have received quantum healing claim that physical to mental and spiritual healing benefits bring many incredible results. Quantum healing often includes a specific breathing practice that supports the body's access to life force energy and encourages greater healing experiences.

Qigong

. . .

Qigong means "vital life force effort." Like Reiki and quantum healing, it works alongside the energy of life force to promote energy healing in the physical body. However, Qigong uses both breathing techniques and meditation practices to stimulate the practice of healing and encourage energetic healing in the body.

Qigong is a self-healing method taught and then personally practiced by people trained in Qigong. You don't have to be trained to practice in Qigong, although it's a good idea to have a trained practitioner to show you how to facilitate self-healing to ensure you use the method properly.

Qigong practitioners sometimes practice what is known as "Qi emission," a Qigong style that helps the practitioner heal your body & energy. These practices are believed to be just as effective, although you need to be around a practitioner to gain access to these healing practices. If you want to use Qigong as an energetic healing method to help you thrive as an Empath in life, learning how to engage in the self-healing method is the best way to ensure that you get the most benefit from Qigong.

. . .

Yoga

Yoga is a practice of physical exercise with deep spiritual roots. Yoga is a practice used to engage the physical body in different positions to stimulate the flow of energy and to support individuals in healing at an energetic or physical level. If you regularly participate in yoga, you ensure that energy flows through you successfully, as you also gain the meditative benefits that promote the flow of energy and life force.

You're probably already familiar with yoga and how people can access this healing method. You can easily participate in yoga by joining in a local class or by following one of the many videos online. You allow yourself to keep your energy body clear and maintain a more peaceful control over the energy flowing into and out of your auric body by engaging in regular yoga practice.

There are many different types of yoga so you can

take advantage of the time you spend studying each type of yoga and considering which one can be most beneficial to you based on your unique energy needs. If you want, you can certainly mix styles, but most forms are designed with a particular style of teaching in mind. In other words, the energetic practices and meditative experiences taught in each style of yoga vary according to where they originate.

You'll probably find overlapping information in each form, but the way it's taught and the methods used to achieve the desired results vary from one style to another.

- Hatha yoga

- Iyengar yoga

- Kundalini yoga

- Ashtanga yoga

- Vinyasa yoga

- Bikram yoga

- Yin yoga

- Prenatal yoga

- Prenatal yoga

- Jivamukti yoga

Each of these styles focuses on spiritual healing in a way that is understandable and accessible to beginning aspiring yogis. None of these practices necessarily require you to position yourself in any way that can be challenging for someone new to yoga. This makes it easy to start with an incredibly supportive to maintain your energy balance and feel confident as an Empath.

6

LEARNING TO CONTROL YOUR ENERGY

*L*earning how to manage your energy is the first part of learning how to heal your energy.

Learning how to control your energy as an Empath gives you the ability to have a greater say in what your energy field enters and how it affects you. This is your opportunity to overcome the feelings of helplessness and the mercy of other energies so you can feel more control and empowerment in your life. In addition to helping you feel a greater sense of empowerment, learning to control your energies will help you recognize something in your energy body quickly.

The moment your energies begin to feel over-whelmed, you can prevent them from building up and causing problems by planning yourself an energy healing session. Ultimately, controlling your energies requires three steps:

1. Identifying your energies
2. Identifying the energies of other people
3. Setting energy limits so that no one else can interrupt your energy field

In this chapter, we'll explore how you can start doing this in your life so you can gain personal control and feel more confident when you enter the world around you. One of the main reasons why Empaths feel vulnerable and overwhelmed is because they struggle to recognize their own energies apart from others' energies.

As a result, they end up feeling that everything comes from within them and they derive a great sense of overwhelm from the difficulty of identifying why or how it happens. When an Empath realizes that many of these energies aren't their own, there can be a great sense of relief. This great sense of relief can then be followed by a sense of frustration that knowledge of how to prevent energy from building up and burdening their energy field is lacking.

If you've ever felt frustrated and overwhelmed by the energies of others, you still haven't learned to discern the difference between your own energies and others. This is the first step in learning how to control your energies so you can avoid being "hijacked" by the energetic experience and feeling of someone else caught at the mercy of those around you. When you learn how to identify your own energies, it becomes easier to identify the energy of others around you.

This can take some time and practice, but the more you practice, the easier it's for you to recognize your energies compared to others.

The best way to start is to:

Identify your own energies

• • •

If you have a stronger sense of who you're and how your personal energy feels, it's easier for you to identify which energies aren't yours. Of course, your own field of energy will change according to your moods and experiences, so that your field of energy may not always feel the same.

For this reason, you should invest some serious time in getting to know your own personal energy so you can build a strong sense of what your energy feels like in different circumstances. It's as simple to identify your own energy as slowing down and tuning into your inner self. It's a great way to identify your energies to spend some time in meditation to identify what energy most resonates with you. Most people report that somewhere around their solar plexus chakra or the core of their physical being they feel their personal energy. It's thought that this is where our personal power comes from, so it makes sense for many people to feel their personal energy.

However, you can feel yours differently, so be sure to tune in and consider what resonates with you. If it's your energy, a great way to tell is to consider the feeling you get when someone says your name. This usually causes a sensation in your body that leads you to hear who is talking to you. The same familiar feeling is the type you feel when you identify your personal energy successfully. It's also a good idea to do small meditative check-ins during the day when different emotions or energies are experienced. This gives you a sense of what your body feels like when you experience different things like anger, fear, joy, gratitude or an excess of energy. At first, you might find it a challenge to discover which energies you know or feel like because, in this sense, you might have spent so much time separating yourself from them.

As you continue to check in and recognize what your own energy feels like, this sense of familiarity continues to grow for you and strengthens your ability to identify your own energies. This way, you can build trust in yourself and your body of energy while telling yourself apart from others. This process alone is a huge step in the right direction for an Empath.

Identifying Other People's Energies

. . .

Once you have successfully identified your own energies, you must begin to identify how it feels when the energy of someone else penetrates your body.

When you learn how to identify the energies of other people, it's even easier for you to draw the barrier between yourself and others in a way that allows you to recognize their own energy and your own energy. You've probably recognized the energies of other people to some extent, even if you don't fully realize it. I bet you can think of a person, for example, who makes you feel "off" the minute they enter the room. Maybe their energy is quite toxic, so whenever they're around you, it's like you can feel the energy in your own space immediately. You might even feel an increased state of fear or overwhelm, probably reflecting the toxic behavior of the person's inner pain.

Similarly, you might think of someone who has a beautiful energy and always makes you feel so comforted and welcomed in their space. You might even want their presence because it helps you to feel so relaxed and comfortable in your own life.

Although not everyone's energy will have such an obvious and profound impact, you can experience the energy of everyone, whether you want it or not. It's until you take control of your own energy.

Learning how to recognize the difference between your energy and someone else's will make it easy for you to establish this boundary and maintain empathy without taking on the experience of the other person physically, mentally, emotionally or spiritually as if it were your own. The first step is to know how to identify your own energy, as this helps you to recognize your own energy immediately. You must then proceed and begin to identify everything that isn't yours, as this will tell you clearly which energies you feel belong to someone else.

The best time to practice this is when you start to feel overwhelmed in a public setting. These are often the types of environments in which the barriers between your energy and the energies of other people can blur, as you have not yet established healthy energy limits.

When you start to feel this overwhelming feeling, you have to act by identifying where the overwhelm comes from. You can do this by checking the same self-awareness checks you used to identify your own energy. First, you need to identify your own energy and develop a sense of familiarity that will help you ground and keep you in your own space strong. You must then identify everything that isn't your own energy, as it will obviously be energy that belongs to someone else. Spend a couple of minutes visualizing the barrier between your energy and the energy of others so you can feel confident that the two differ. This will help you feel a stronger sense of self that gives you the courage and trust you need to control your own energy field. You can take action in two ways once you have identified the barrier between yourself and others.

First, you can act by requesting that any energy that isn't yours inherently be removed from your energy field so that you can resume your own natural energy state. This will ensure that all energies that have penetrated your borders are removed from your field to promote a sense of trust and calm in your own energy.

The second thing you need to do is set energetic

boundaries. These energy limits will ensure that other people's energy doesn't penetrate your energy field regularly. This doesn't mean you won't feel and recognize their energy, but it doesn't mean it can create a feeling that you're attacked by other people's energy.

Creating energy boundaries is a healthy and empowering way to protect yourself from the energies of other people without closing yourself completely away from those around you. When using energy limits, you ensure that the energetic exchange between you and someone else doesn't exceed what you feel comfortable and reasonable. For example, if you're in the presence of someone with toxic energy, your energy boundary would insist that your toxic energy doesn't penetrate your energy field. As a result, you could still see their toxic energies, but they wouldn't feel as if they were attacking you personally or entering your sacred personal space. This can help you overcome the experience of taking on the energies and emotions of other people as if they were your own.

The same way you create physical or personal

boundaries, you can generate energy boundaries. Start by identifying where the border is and what it should be. For example, if you feel overwhelmed by negative energy, you can set the limit that the negative energy of other people can no longer be *your* negative energy. Setting the boundary is as simple as declaring it and becoming aware of that boundary, the harder part is your need to maintain that boundary. To support the boundary and assert it as necessary, you must either verbally or energetically assert it to others, as well as maintain it with yourself. When it comes to bringing negative energy into your space to other people, you can approach the situation in the way you think it will be most effective.

If the person behaves in a toxic way, it can be most useful to address the situation and verbalize your border. If they're unaware of their toxicity or seem to behave reasonably kindly, but their energy is still toxic, it may be more appropriate to assert an energetic limit. What this means is that you assert to yourself and your energy field that no toxic energies will be accepted into your space, and then you uphold this assertion by not allowing their energy to impact you further. It's also essential to stick to the boundaries. Many people believe that the only boundaries to be established are those between them-selves and others, but this isn't the case. If you and yourself set a boundary, break it to yourself or to others. You claim that this limit doesn't matter and that energy can freely leak through it, as you won't prevent it.

This means that if you claim you don't want toxic energy in your space, you can't become toxic to others or yourself. You must work to set the limits and remove all toxic behaviors, thoughts, and words from your life when you interact with yourself or anyone else. Your boundaries are thus kept healthy, and you can continue to grow.

Why You Need To Stop Shielding Yourself

Many Empathic resources advocate the benefits of shielding yourself, and they're right to some extent. However, keeping a constant shield over yourself is both ineffective and counterintuitive to what you as a healing Empath are trying to achieve. If you put a shield between yourself and those around you, you try to ensure that all energy remains entirely out and that your own energy remains entirely in it. This means that you don't experience positive and pleasant things in such a pleasant way because you try to keep everything out. It also means you have trouble interacting with your own environment and enjoying it. Also, holding this shield can be exhausting and can add to the many reasons why Empaths often want to live an entirely introverted life.

Another disadvantage of shields is that whenever you engage with your environment, you produce an energetic "leak" in the shield, which means that any energy can enter or exit the shield freely because there's now space where the shield isn't maintained. For any Empath, this can be a very overwhelming and frustrating experience, especially one who can only understand his or her own gifts.

If you've ever found yourself trying to hold a shield, but feeling exhausted or struggling to make it "work," it's because they don't work in many cases. Shields are great for moments when you don't want energy to come in or out in a particularly toxic environment. However, the shield just won't be enough for your average outing or social experience. The creation of energetic boundaries as I outlined above is the best way for an Empath to engage in a social environment without feeling the intensely adverse effects of the energies surrounding it.

Through these boundaries, the Empath can feel protected and separate from everyone else and feel as if they can genuinely enjoy and engage in the environment around them. Boundaries are the most powerful tool you can use as an Empath because they provide all the protection you want from your shield without any energy leaks or exhaustion.

DESIGNING YOUR HEALING DREAM

or you to immediately begin to experience relief from your empathy, it's essential to create a healing dream learning to control your energies and engage in energetic healing. If you want to undertake Empathic healing, however, you need to start focusing on how you can create a long-term healing goal that will allow you to thrive in your life. The best way to do this is to build a dream and learn how to integrate it into your real life. In this chapter, we'll explore how you can develop your healing dream so that healing and prosperity can truly be incorporated into your life.

This is an essential practice for anyone who wants to experience long-term healing, so ensure you engage in this practice for some time. Because you're an Empath, your already lively inner world is likely to have a lot of fun engaging and using this practice as a way to create a healing experience for yourself!

The importance of a healing dream

Empaths who have not yet fully embraced the path of healing and living as a confident and prosperous Empath can still feel as if they're condemned to a lifetime of overwhelming experience and struggle to protect themselves. This can be an exhausting and dreary outlook that can make everyone, especially someone who is sensitive and feels things so profoundly, looks forward to an enjoyable life challenging. Creating a healing dream for yourself gives you the chance to dream of a life you'd love to live, regardless of what your Empathic self feels right now.

If you dream of being outgoing and committed to the world around you, it's essential to incorporate this into your dream. If you dream of traveling alone and staying mostly alone, it's also necessary to include this. Your dream's real goal is to identify your true innermost desires and give yourself hope that they can become a real experience for you. Empaths often learn to live their whole lives around their gifts, sometimes even giving up parts of their authentic self to avoid feeling overwhelmed and exhausted.

You want your dream to help you learn how to live your life and to be an Empath in your life. The big difference here is that a person allows his gift to rule his life in the former experience, and in the latter experience that person takes control and rules his own life. Your dream is about creating a real visual of yourself living your best life so that you can make this vision your goal. This is your vision you'll hold on to so that you can begin to heal and overcome the problems that have held you back so far. Whenever you struggle to move forward or to recover, this vision will help you to find out what next steps need to be taken so that you can evolve in a way that includes healing your fears and regaining control.

How to design your healing dream

Creating your healing dream is as easy as sitting with your daydreams and dreaming about what you want to happen in your life. However, because you want this dream to remain somewhat consistent and eventually come true, it's vital that you take a few additional steps to help you make this dream come true.

These steps include: becoming very specific, writing down your dream so that you can revisit it as often as you want, and releasing the result so that you can still feel fulfilled by what you have manifested if your dream is realized in a way that looks different from what you expected.

Clarifying your vision

If you clarify your vision, you can see it and be excited about it. This also gives you something clear and specific to work towards, which is an essential part of making a dream a goal. When you dream without being particular, many variables leave room for you to aim for what you want or know if you're making progress. To clarify your dream, you have to spend some time thinking about who, when, where, why and how. Look to make your vision as real as possible when you clarify it. See if you can make your dream so clear that it almost feels like a memory for something that has already happened, rather than a dream.

This will help your mind to honestly see you live your life in this way, which will help you to manifest your dream life. When your mind can truly see and feel how successful it looks, it mentally prepares you for the changes you make and the challenges you face along the way. This is a powerful way to ensure success. In addition to dreaming up your vision, writing it down can also be helpful. Writing your vision in your journal or on a piece of paper and keeping it close is a great way to review the vision regularly.

It also makes it feel much more real as if you're writing a goal rather than just a dream. This helps you to alchemize your dream energy by transitioning it from the energy of longing to the energy of creation. The very act of writing down your vision also gives you the chance to validate yourself and your life's desires.

Many people create dreams, but then surround those dreams with negative beliefs or ideas that because of various reasons or excuses they create for themselves, they can not possibly bring those dreams into their reality. Writing your dream down allows you to approve yourself and validate your wishes so you can start building a sense of trust in your dream. This will help you change your hope into faith, so you'll go from hoping it's true to having faith. Release the result This may seem counterintuitive, but it's also important to release the result of your dream. The reason for this is that what we want in life often appears in ways we couldn't have expected. Your dreams will heal and evolve as you heal and grow.

This means that any dreams you might have held that were the product of the desires of someone else will be slowly released from your psyche and replaced by your real dreams and desires. It also means that as you evolve, you might be exposed to new information that calls you in a different direction from what you dreamed of. Allowing yourself to release the result ensures you remain subscribed to a dream that truly serves you and your wishes. Trying to heal yourself by forcing yourself to stay adhered to a dream you have made in the past will only hold you back, as this old dream won't help you at that moment to feel your best. Be prepared to release the result and allow the dream to reflect what you honestly want in your life.

You'll then find yourself living the best possible life. Apart from giving you faith and direction, effectively using your healing dream, your dream gives you the opportunity to start taking practical steps towards the life you want to live. You can use your dream to begin to make the next best move, to help you feel the way you want to feel and to encourage you to stay on track at all times.

Your dream is a powerful guide that can give you all you need to move forward and live your best life when used correctly. When it comes to practically using your dream, try to use it as a compass for your life and the choices you make in your life. Look at your dream and consult it whenever you struggle in your life to take action, change or make a choice. If you feel stuck, pray for your dream to guide you to your next step so that you can continue to achieve what you want in life.

If you feel doubtful in your dream or in yourself, spend some time visualizing your wishes and empowering your vision and filling you with faith and direction. To keep your dream practical, ensure you spend time actively allowing it to evolve. Whenever you notice that your dream doesn't resonate fully with you, spend some time considering what aspects of your dream don't resonate. This will help you keep your dream "up to date" so you don't get caught in an old dream.

THE HEALING OF YOUR PAST

*E*mpaths are often affected by their past experiences, which can lead to a negative ongoing approach to every day life. For example: an Empath who has experienced a traumatic narcissistic relationship may feel extremely co-dependent and struggle to live a "normal" life due to someone else's damage. This is true for anyone who has experienced trauma, but it can be especially challenging or harmful for Empaths who tend to internalize things and feel the trauma in a way that others can't.

You've probably experienced many bigger and smaller traumas in your own life that have made you feel like you need healing. As an Empath, you have probably been exposed to more traumatic experiences or events than other people. This is because the internalization of energy and emotions can be traumatic, leading to experiences that can be "normal" for Empaths. It's also because other people tend to recognize that Empaths are vulnerable and take advantage of empathy either consciously or subconsciously. You're more susceptible to adverse experiences like narcissists and energy vampires as an Empath.

Healing your past experiences will allow you to end the cycle of others taking control of you and give you the chance to retake control of yourself. When you combine the healing of your past with the process of taking control of your own energy, you create a powerful person. Your ability to feel confident and strong in yourself and to feel tender and compassionate towards others in a way that doesn't harm yourself is a mixture that allows you to heal the collective without draining your energy whilst doing so.

Identify your life lessons

By identifying your life lessons, you can significantly improve your healing experience. Life lessons are lessons that take root early in our childhood and appear through patterns we experience in our lives time and time again. Each person has his or her own unique life lessons to be learned, although your life lessons may overlap with the experiences of others.

Identifying your life lessons will help you learn and integrate these lessons into your life so that you can start living with a healthier and controlled approach to life. It will also help you understand why certain types of energy can affect you more than others, causing your Empathic gifts to feel overwhelmed when you're out. Whenever you experience some-one's energy that triggers your life lesson, it leaves a lasting impact far greater than any of the other ener-gies you experience. These energies left unmanaged, can be extremely overwhelming and frustrating.

The easiest way to identify what your life lessons could be is to look back over your lifetime of experi-ences and consider what patterns you see in your traumatic or challenging experiences. Identifying the patterns, you experience in your life will help you to discover what you might need to learn. It's important to understand that it takes more time and self-aware-ness to understand what this lesson is, as these lessons are often buried in our subconscious mind until we address them, evaluate them and integrate them. Once you have a general understanding of what these patterns are, take them for their face value and consider their lessons. For example, if you have been consistently surrounded by narcissists in your past, your experience can be to learn how to detect and protect yourself against narcissists.

This is a great opportunity to begin to integrate your life lessons and overcome these challenges so that you can once again take control of your life. However, you must continue to look at this trigger or lesson to see how specific you can get, realizing that life lessons aren't always obvious. Ask yourself questions like "how do I attract narcissists? "how can I fight to protect myself from this? "or" why am I in this situation vulnerable? "you can learn more about your unique circumstances. You might find that the underlying lesson is that you need to be more compassionate about yourself and your own needs, or that you need to stop trying to overlap and "save" others ' lives.

Identifying these life lessons and getting into the root of what they are, why they're there and how they can be learned will help you feel a stronger sense of control in your life. Instead of feeling deeply triggered by something and not knowing completely why or feeling haunted by a particular type of energy in your life, you can begin to take control and integrate this lesson so that these triggers or energies no longer bother you. As an Empath, this type of self-awareness and personal control changes your life by allowing you to stop feeling so overwhelmed by the energies around you. Healing your past and understanding your experiences are great ways to experience self-confidence and a better life.

How you can heal your past

The lessons of your life have been deeply embedded in your past and have probably had a massive impact on your life. For some Empaths, their life lessons can completely change their personality until they can integrate and learn from the lessons. An Empath who has been extroverted as a child, for example, but has endured many lessons that echo the same purpose, may be overwhelmed and anxious, leading them to live life as an introvert to avoid pain.

It's imperative to heal your past, as it will help you access your true self so that you can stop living as a victim of your past and embrace your gifts. Your past can be healed in many ways, although a healthy mix of approaches is usually required to ensure that you're thoroughly healed. It can also take a while to dive into previous trauma, discomfort, pain and suffering experiences as a way to relieve this pain and move forward in your life. Together with someone who can offer you compassionate support without interrupting your healing process, this is usually best.

Ideally, this should be a therapist who can help you

with practices like talk therapy, although in many cases a trusted friend would also work well. I've listed five practices below that you can begin to release and heal from these past hurts. Make the decision to let it go Before you can heal anything, you have to make the decision to let it go. Getting into the mindset of letting things go allows you to move from the position of holding on to your pain so you can move forward.

We often want to let something go from our past, but we can't or don't want to make that desire a decision so we can do it. What happens is that, even if we want to move forward, we sit with that pain and continue to see ourselves as victims of the experiences we've had. In the end, we're the only person who continues to suffer. To make the decision, you just have to agree that you're ready to let go of your experience.

This doesn't mean that the experience is in any way reduced, invalidated or considered "OK" but rather that you're willing to accept it for what it's and move forward knowing that it can not be changed. You find the opportunity to begin true healing on yourself and in your life in this acceptance and willingness. Express your pain Now that you have decided to let go of your pain, you must try to express your pain. If you try to let something go without expressing the pain you have felt, you'll find yourself struggling to let it go, because there are still many repressed emotions.

Allowing yourself to feel the pain and express it productively helps you to move the energy out of yourself to continue your healing path. This is your essential step as an Empath to ensure that you no longer hold on to so many different overwhelming energies in your body of energy. You give yourself the opportunity to start from a clean slate by releasing these energies. You won't feel so quickly and easily overwhelmed anymore, because you won't try to take more energies on top of all those you already hold on to. You have to take responsibility for your experience in choosing to let go of something.

This means that you no longer choose to remain in the victim's mentality where you blame the other person for taking responsibility for your life and experience. This doesn't mean you take the blame for the wrongdoings of someone else or your own consequences. Instead, it means you choose to take responsibility for the healing process and let go of what you have done. This very process of taking responsibility moves you out of the mentality of the victim and helps you to take control of your life.

Empaths have a strong tendency to live in a victim's mentality when they still have to take control of themselves and their energy, which often leads to the belief that Empathic gifts are a curse. This is because you don't know how to take responsibility for yourself and your experiences. In this way, you can experience liberation from your difficult experiences so that you can start to experience a better life.

Concentrate on the present

After you chose to let go, expressed all your emotions and took responsibility for yourself and your choices, you completed everything you had to do with the past. You have to start focusing on the present and how you can improve your current life. This is an excellent opportunity for you to start considering the consequences of your painful experiences and how it's shaped your life ever since. You can also look at your Empathic gifts and find how your experience can make you feel some emotions stronger than others when it comes to emotionally and energetically taking over the experiences of other people. In many cases, you'll find that your most common emotions are directly related to previous painful experiences in your own life.

When you choose to live in the present, think about how you can start living your life in a more authentic and fulfilling way. Seek the chance to find out how you can continue to overcome the effects of your past pains so that you can live in a way that feels good for you. Choose to live in the healing light all the time. Whenever you experience something that would have triggered you as a result of that previous experience, make the conscious effort to let go and move forward in your life at that moment. The final step in healing is to forgive yourself and forgive anyone who has hurt you in your past.

Pardon is your opportunity to take control of your present and prevent your past self and people from your past from further hurting you. You might find that in some cases, forgiveness requires a regular commitment so that you and others can truly remain in forgiveness. It's essential that you honor the process of forgiveness, no matter how you look, so you can continue to feel free from your past pains. Forgiveness is truly a liberating experience as an Empath.

When you forgive, you alchemize the painful energy

of the awareness of the victim and take control of yourself and your life again. This is the step in which you actually clear the residual energy of the past so that you don't feel like you're continually trying to approach life from a cup that is already overflowing with stress and overwhelming. Instead, you can approach life clearly and freely from your past with the ability to see things.

9

HEALING YOUR INNER CHILD

*A*lthough you have already begun to heal your past, another key action is needed if you're to experience true and complete healing in your life. As an Empath, addressing your inner child and healing this part of yourself is an important part of healing. While healing your past will help to heal your inner child, other actions should be taken to support your inner child in healing fully. Your inner child is the part of you that still sees the past as if it lives in the past, and not in the present through your more experienced and understanding eyes. That's why it needs to be healed as an adult, regardless of your past healing. Healing your inner child is an incredibly liberating experience for many Empaths that support them in feeling truly and completely free from their past troubles.

. . .

This is the chance to completely overcome that small inner voice that continues to cry "danger" every time you see a trigger that even remotely reflects an example you have had in the past. By healing your inner child, every time you go to a social event or find yourself in a public space, you can stop feeling so on edge. When your inner child is healed, she no longer feels so concerned and afraid of the world around her that he can approach life in a calmer state. As a result, it becomes much easier to address and deal with any energy you might face in your life. For anyone who wants complete healing in their lives, healing your inner child is important, but it's especially important for Empaths.

Since you have been highly sensitive throughout your life, you might have plenty of memories to remember where you felt the impact of your sensitivities. The way people spoke to you, the energy they had when they spoke to you and even the energy of the environments you visited would have left a lasting impression on your mind as you grew up. This means that you have to consider even more healing than the average person who hasn't experienced higher levels of sensitivity throughout his life. The first step in healing your inner child is actually accessing your inner child so that you can start sharing communications with this part of yourself.

You can think of your inner child as a small voice within you that still thinks, talks and acts like a child, even though you're an adult now. For example, if you're angry and that inner part of you begin to experience the feelings of a temper tantrum, even if your adult realizes that a temper tantrum isn't a valid or productive response to your anger. Your inner child reflects this inner part of you, which still wants to respond to situations in a more emotional and less rational sense.

To access your inner child, you need to take the time to recognize that it exists and needs to be addressed. Allowing yourself to become aware of this need and to recognize it as a valid and important part of yourself helps you to provide your inner child with the safe space in which it needs to emerge. You have to start talking to your inner child. Talking to your inner child allows you to give her the attention he needs while understanding why she feels and acts the way she is. This is the very information you'll use to heal so you can start feeling emotional freedom and stop feeling so overwhelmed by your sensitivity.

Some people who are more attracted to the use of physical objects or their environment as a way to engage in mental and spiritual practices may find that it's easier to access their inner child if they have something from childhood. For example, looking at a picture of your younger self or sitting with a teddy bear in your childhood can stimulate your inner child and encourage him or her to come out and spend some time sharing. If you don't have your childhood belongings, you can always collect an object that looks like something you had in your childhood. Once you recognize and access this energy, you can start talking to your inner child and ask him questions. Some great questions to begin with include: "How are you? "or" what do you want me to know now?". This encourages this part of your psyche to start talking to you and to share information about how it can respond to the world around you.

. . .

For Empaths, this part of yourself probably has a lot of fear and anxiety about your adult experiences. It's a powerful way to start the healing process so your inner child can stop feeling traumatized by the world around you.

How to gain the trust of your inner child

You must gain the trust of your inner child if you want to embrace the healing process of your inner child fully. Many Empaths find that their inner child feels betrayed, abandoned, neglected or simply forgotten. This is because most people don't realize that their inner child still exists and needs support to understand and overcome life's challenges. Whenever you endure a new challenge in life or embrace it, your inner child will still respond in the same way as your childhood.

You still have an inner part of you that struggles to see, understand and respond to the world around you, despite the evolution you have endured. This part of you wants those around you and yourself to love, respect, cherish and appreciate. She also wants you to show her affection and be compassionate and tender, often reflecting something you might never have experienced fully as a child.

In life, our inner child often feels abandoned and

neglected if she's not given the tender compassion and love she needs in these sensitive moments, especially as an Empath. As an adult, your inner child will naturally still respond immediately to these feelings, even if you don't recognize it or become aware of it. That's why your inner child has grown to see you as untrustworthy. It's therefore important to gain your inner child's trust. As an Empath, your inner child is likely to feel wounded because she continues to worry that she's "too sensitive" or "too serious." This part of you still stings each time someone tells you that you need to grow a thicker skin or recognizes a joke when you hear one, even if it doesn't sound funny to you.

Although you're now more aware of these experiences or more compassionate about yourself and your sensitivity, your inner child still longs for this tenderness and compassion. You can gain your inner child's trust by showing that you recognize that it still exists and that you're willing to acknowledge it and remain aware of it. By teaching your inner child that you have not forgotten them, but rather that you have not realized that they're still there, you can ask for pardon from your inner child and then work to gain their trust. In doing so, you bring your inner child more comfort. Trust your inner childhood self that you, yourself, are there for them now and want to listen to them, see them and support them in their experiences.

You must be incredibly tender and gentle with yourself and be consistent and devoted so that your inner child can see that you're serious about supporting it. If your inner child has been repressed for a long time, it may take some time to gain confidence and be able to fully access and listen to it. Be patient and continue to listen to your inner child so you can show that you're trustworthy. The more you do this, the more your inner child opens up to you and shares its feelings and experiences. This will help you to understand your own emotions deeply and why you're so sensitive to specific experiences as opposed to others or more sensitive to all experiences in general. Once you have accessed your inner child's trust and gained it, you can start working to heal it. The best way to begin healing your inner child is to express the emotions your inner child feels.

Allow all these feelings during these conversations to rise to the surface and be expressed wholly and healthily. If you have fear, let yourself shake it out. If you want to cry because you feel sad or shame, let it come out too. Use this opportunity to feel and release any emotion that wishes to rise to the surface. When you express the emotions that your inner child hasn't had the chance to communicate fully, you allow yourself to release the energy that this memory or experience entangles. This allows you to completely release the inner "bottle" that has filled over the years and restore a peaceful and calm state within you. When you release these emotions, you might feel anxious about the intensity of the emotions that arise.

You might be worried that these emotions will be overwhelming or you won't be able to control them. Trust that this isn't the case and that even when your emotions come out, you'll still be able to experience full control. This fear belongs to your inner child, and it's worried that she'll lose control because she was told it was wrong to lose control. Now you're an adult who can stay in control while expressing your emotions so that you don't have to worry about this experience. Just let the fear be expressed and then your other emotions will be experienced. You can thus experience a complete release of your emotions and release the incredible amount of energy associated with them. Your inner child is likely to express only a few things at a time.

After all, you have been a child for many years so you might need to recognize and express many years of experience. As you continue to work with this practice, each time you feel a greater sense of release.

You might find that your inner child is satisfied over time and you no longer need to engage in such healing practices. When this happens, you should see that your ability to process life as an Empath is also much more natural, as you now have more control over yourself, your energies and your emotions.

10

HEALING YOUR PRESENT SELF

The next step in your healing journey is to understand and heal your present self. Healing your present self is an opportunity for you to release anything that can cause energetic or emotional turmoil in your life right now so you can truly enjoy life. Most of the time, healing your current self requires you to consider what your current state of well-being is and start healing towards your own vision. Healing your past and inner child will help you feel released from the attachments that have held you in this state, but healing your present self will allow you to release the symptoms caused by your past entirely.

The healing of the present self enables Empaths to begin to experience a greater sense of self-confidence and self-esteem so that they can start to enjoy life from a more intentional and empowered point of view. We'll explore in this chapter how healing your current self can improve your life and how you can use your better self-esteem and self-confidence to experience a better life as an Empath. Even if you're someone who already considers your self-esteem and confidence to be reasonably high, working on this healing practice will ensure that you use this strong sense of self in the best possible way to support your inner Empath.

Identifying What Needs To Be Healed

Before you can start to heal your current self, you must first consider what might be wrong. Looking into your past makes it easy to see trauma or challenges, as you can now see how they affected your life. Looking at your present life and trying to consider what may "go wrong" can be much more challenging because these are the behaviors, thoughts, and experiences you actively engage in. To determine what needs to be healed, it's useful to spend some time writing down the things you want to be changed or improved about your current life. Consider everything from communicating with others and yourself to dealing with different situations in your life. All these experiences contain massive amounts of energy that can affect your energy and make the world around you feel vulnerable or overwhelming.

When you talk about what needs to be healed, don't be afraid to consider parts of yourself that may have been affected by past experiences, even if you have already deliberately worked to heal these past experiences. Our past experiences often lead to current problems that must also be addressed. Just because you healed the pain memory doesn't mean that your behavior, thoughts, and attitude at this time still doesn't last. Addressing the present self, which also needs healing, will help you to fully heal from past experiences so that you can move forward and start living a better life completely free from all attachments to the past. You'll probably find many things to some extent that need to be addressed or healed. Even that won't end. Healing is an ongoing process that needs to be addressed and worked on regularly to ensure that you stay at your highest energy level.

Regular self-reflection and journaling are the best way to ensure that you always identify aspects of yourself that can be healed. This will help you to remain self-aware and fully committed to your practice of healing.

The importance of self-awareness

If you're not a self-aware person, self-healing can be a difficult process. To be able to heal yourself requires you to look into yourself and notice the parts of yourself that need healing. As an Empath, self-awareness tends to come naturally and inevitably help you on your healing journey.

You might also find, however, that if you live in the archetype of a "cursed" Empath, you have long suppressed your feelings and self-esteem. Some Empaths even report body experiences or dissociation experiences as a way to detach themselves from the painful experiences of empathy. In these circumstances, it may be more difficult for you to achieve self-awareness. If you don't already live in a state of self-awareness, you'll want to start practicing so you can understand yourself and your needs more clearly.

The best way to start practicing self-awareness is to check in regularly and ask yourself how you do something. Asking yourself such questions requires you to check your feelings, thoughts, and needs and then take care of yourself. This creates a strong relationship between you and yourself that helps you feel worthy of your time and attention. Like the healing of the inner child, you might find that you must work to gain your own trust to embrace the art of self-awareness fully.

Continue to show compassion and tenderness, and you'll probably find that self-awareness naturally comes from this growing relationship you share with yourself. Now that you have brought your desire for healing into your current state of awareness, you can start the process of truly healing these experiences. Since your previous traumas have cultivated all your current problems, you must finally release all your current links to the past. The best way to imagine this process is to consider the experience as weed removal. Your past and inner child's healing allowed you to heal the roots of the problem.

You must now remove the rest of the plant that grew out of those roots to make the person you are today.

Releasing The Final Bonds of Your Past

While you have an idea why you behave in a way that can help you to have a greater sense of understanding, it's not necessary. What is needed is that you address every part of yourself that needs healing and begin to understand why it no longer serves you and how it can be changed to serve you better.

For example, if you find that you tend to be overwhelmed by certain energies even if you have to deal with them regularly, you can set your intention to heal your response around these energies. You can also determine how you want to behave in addition to setting this intention. Using your dream of healing is a great way to help you heal your present self. Through your healing dream, you can "see" how you would prefer to behave and begin to behave in this way. This visualization will help you gradually swap your current manners with new ones that will help you to realize your healing dream.

The process of changing these old behaviors is the last tie of the past that you officially cut loose. After this change, you'll feel like you're completely liberated from the experience that once held you in an energetic and emotional turmoil. This release allows you to feel more confident about yourself and your ability to assert your boundaries, including your energetic boundaries so that you can regain control of your life and stop feeling as if you're victimized by your Empathic gifts.

Incorporating regular self-healing

It's important that you understand that healing is an ongoing experience. You'll never be completely "healed" because more can always be addressed, evaluated and improved. If you want to embrace healing, you must be willing to embrace the full journey, no matter how long it is. Some parts of the process can be difficult, painful or just frustrating. Other parts may feel like you've been waiting far too long for the healing and you're excited to overcome your problems and start living a better life. In the end, your version that has undergone more healing sincerely appreciates your efforts. If you want to embrace a healing journey, incorporating your healing into your regular routine is a requirement.

Regular self-reflection, journaling, and dreaming are the best way to do this. The more you recognize unhealed parts of yourself and dream what it would be like to heal them, the easier it will be for you to visualize and then manifest yourself living your best life. As an Empath, using healing energy in this way gives you great freedom from the overwhelming sensitivity that can lead you.

11

PRACTICING SOCIAL HEALING

*E*mpaths are rarely fully appreciated and accepted by our modern society as the world at large tends not to understand and appreciate the struggles of a highly sensitive person. Unfortunately, as an Empath in every day life, it may not always be well received to express your sensitive side. This can make you feel like you're not welcome in society. This can further aggravate your inner feelings of abandonment and neglect and lead to internal emotional trauma from your "broken" relationship with others in general. Learning how to heal your social experiences can help you engage in social experiences at a higher level so that you can begin to enjoy the public or the experiences you need to go out in public.

In this chapter, we'll explore how you can heal the

feeling that society is outcast so that you can start to enjoy a better life and feel genuinely fulfilled in every possible way. Whether you're a shy or an extroverted Empath, these practices will help to support your healing.

Taking full responsibility for yourself

The first step towards better social experiences is to take responsibility for yourself. Learning how to take responsibility for your energy and experience helps you stay clear of the mentality of being the victim. This prevents you from feeling as if you're being attacked continuously whenever you go in public because you can choose to avoid these feelings of energetic attacks. When you realize that you're not disliked by society and that you're entirely welcomed into the world as it's, it becomes much easier for you to stop taking everything personally. You can stop feeling like you have the energies of everyone else and you have to take responsibility for them.

One of the worst beliefs to hold as an Empath is that you're responsible for any energies or emotions in your space. That's not true. Only your own energies and emotions are your responsibility. If they're affected or influenced by the energies or emotions of someone else, it's your responsibility to *recognize* this and adjust your approach to the situation to avoid negative energy or an emotional experience that is unwanted.

When you take responsibility for yourself, it becomes much easier to stop taking responsibility for others who help you to enforce your energy boundaries so that you no longer accept emotions or energies that aren't yours.

Overcoming the "sponge" belief

An unfortunate belief that the some communities circulate is that Empaths are "sponges" that constantly "soak up" the emotions and energies of other people. This is certainly what it can feel when you don't take care of yourself and your energies actively, but once you start, this symptom disappears, meaning that you don't have to feel like a sponge forever. Believing that you'll always be a sponge that constantly absorbs other people's energies and emotions can be extremely easy to believe, given that you felt it in the past and that others strengthen your feeling.

However, it becomes much easier for you to stop absorbing the energies of everyone else when you choose to take responsibility for yourself and your energies and start practicing and enforcing your energetic boundaries. It's important that you choose to foster a new belief as soon as possible so that your feelings of absorption don't continue to be reinforced.

The more you repeat this belief, the more you reinforce the meaninglessness of your boundaries, because energy simply passes through. In other words, you make your borders meaningless because you ignore them alone and allow yourself to feel unwanted energies. You need to take responsibility and get rid of the belief that anyone that isn't you has any control over your energies whatsoever.

Take responsibility for your relationship with society

Chances are that your inner child is the part of you who still lives in the fear and shame of society. This means that you're likely to need some healing about society and other people with your inner child. You also need to consider yourself as an adult and how you feel about society at the moment. If your feelings about society are negative, for example: you think everyone is too harsh and nobody appreciates or understands you, you'll strengthen this negative belief and struggle in society, no matter what. If you choose to adjust your beliefs and see society as a beautiful opportunity to connect with others and perhaps meet people who are sensitive like you, society suddenly becomes much less frightening and much more enjoyable.

You allow yourself to heal from those inner feelings associated with being an outcast or someone who was too weak for society when you adjust your beliefs in this way. You give yourself your freedom in healing your relationship with society.

Whether we like it or not, we live in a society and live in disagreement with the world will never help you feel better. If anything, it can make you feel exceptionally vulnerable to the energy of those around you, as you're constantly focused on others' judgmental, rude and harmful energies. As a result, each time you go out in public, your Empathic self will feel extremely overwhelmed. However, if you see society as an opportunity or a simple fact of life, these energies will cease to be so intimidating or frightening to you, and you can enjoy society easily and to it's fullest.

Allowing yourself to have fun

Empaths often struggle to have fun in ways that aren't directly linked to being alone or doing some-thing silent and withdrawn. Although there's nothing wrong with being an introvert or preferring to read or watch a film, rather than being with a group of people, it's not effective if you're the type of person who only chooses books or films because of your fear of society. If the constant worry of going out and enjoying yourself prevents you from actually going out and doing it, you need to learn how to completely detach yourself from the world around you so you can let go and have fun.

At first glance, this may seem impossible, but it is possible, and it can help you live a more fulfilling and happy life. It ultimately requires a commitment to yourself to allow yourself to have fun. In this commitment, you must ensure that you don't worry about the energies or emotions of those around you in a way that makes you feel overwhelmed or responsible for your experience.

Although you can certainly recognize their energies or emotions, allow yourself to completely detach yourself from them so that you can no longer feel their energies as your own. Then, just try to focus on enjoying yourself and the world around you without feeling so overwhelmed and exhausted.

At first, this might seem like an impossible task. It probably sounds difficult to detach yourself, because you might be worried that detachment will prevent you from feeling any emotions whatsoever. I can assure you that that is not the case. Cultivating a healthy detachment will allow you to separate yourself from feeling *personally* responsible for someone else. Among other emotions, you can still experience and express empathy, but you won't feel such a nagging and overwhelming need to engage in energies and emotions that aren't yours.

It can be beneficial for you to start practicing this type of detachment in environments that aren't so overwhelming at first, so you can get the hang of it.. As you do, continue to increase the intensity of your environment at a rate that feels comfortable to you, so that you can fully embrace your detachment at each "level" until you feel confident and ready to move up. Moving at your own pace will help you feel more confident about your control of yourself and your ability to detach yourself from your intense energies.

Advocating for yourself

If you want to be more involved in society as an Empath, being an advocate for yourself is essential. When acting as your own personal advocate, you must pay attention to your needs and wishes whenever you're out and about in public. This is part of your responsibility, but it's also an essential component to your healing that requires your own independent attention.

If you're an advocate for yourself, you must be prepared not only to identify your needs and wishes, but also to ensure that they're met. For example, if you feel particularly overwhelmed by your environment and feel like you need to step out for a few minutes, or excuse yourself from the event so that you can retreat to a more relaxed environment. It's never too big or too an issue small to address, no matter what your need is. It's never too unreasonable to ask – put yourself *first*.

If you spend time with someone who doesn't respect your right to express your own emotions and actively fulfill your needs, you may want to consider spending time with people who may be more concerned about you and your wishes. Ultimately, you're responsible for ensuring that your own needs are met, regardless of who you're with or what attitude they may have. You must ensure that you are an advocate for yourself and your needs at all times so that you can stay confident and be more optimistic about your outings.

AFTERWORD

Congratulations on completing this first step in your journey of self-discovery. I genuinely hope you have discovered more about yourself by reading this book and experience a greater sense of self-awareness through the explanations in this book.

By understanding yourself to a greater extent, you give yourself the power to take control of your own life and to experience a higher quality of life in general. You won't feel like you're living at the mercy of those around you anymore, the more you practice taking control of your life.

You'll find yourself, as an Empath, picking up energies that other people may not even realize. Experiencing these energies when the person responsible for the energies doesn't even want to experience them is a burden that nobody has to take. You must learn to take responsibility for yourself and heal the parts of you that led you to believe otherwise to live your best life. By healing these parts of yourself, you allow yourself to empty the "reserve" of unhealed energies within you so that you can approach life with a greater sense of personal power and trust. You'll access to your best life through that. After reading this book, it's essential that you continue to master your empathic gift.

The more you heal and take your power back while strengthening your personal energy, the easier it will be for you to master your gift. You can then step into your real calling to be a healer, teacher, caretaker or whichever profession feels like it resonates with you the most.

If you can accept this call from a place of power, you'll begin to discover ways in which your empathic gift can genuinely help you rather than hinder you from complete success. Any Empath who tries to embrace their true calling without mastering the gift of being an Empath will quickly feel burnt out by following their passion.

This can lead to a myriad of new problems, including the need to experience further healing, especially around their desires, in their lives. To avoid burnout and exhaustion, first, master the art of empathy and accept your true calling!

12

BOOK TWO

The Enneagram Journey:

Finding The Road Back to the Spirituality Within You - The Made Easy Guide to the 9 Sacred Personality Types: For Healthy Relationships in Couples

INTRODUCTION TO THE ENNEAGRAM

Most of us go through life trying to cope with our own struggles, challenges, and demands unaware of the fact that there's a difference between the real self and the ego self of your personality dealing with everyday life. "Being yourself" is easier said than done in our society because we are often embroiled in mass consciousness and the status quo, leaving little room for authentic self-expression and self-understanding. Enter: the Enneagram. It's a tool designed to help you simplify and increase your self-knowledge and transcend your present level of human consciousness in the process.

In a world of illusions, where everyone wears a mask daily, those who have become tired of masquerades are thirsty for truth and authentic self-expression.

This is not something new; for centuries now the quest has been going on. There have always been those who have been searching for the real knowledge of who they are since Socrates' time and further back. In our society, however, something is changing.

Humanity is making a momentous leap in consciousness by experiencing the need to develop higher, better, more detailed thinking and behaviours to cope with as our lives become more complex. However, what most of us are discovering is that this approach doesn't work too well.

The best way to thrive as the world continues to make a global shift is not to look for more complicated coping mechanisms to tackle the new emerging world, but rather to simplify the way we relate and partner with life. In other words, we realize that seeking simple solutions to our complex problems is the best option. We're learning to prioritize and appreciate this quest for truth, and we've become curious to find out if there's more to us than we've grown up to believe about ourselves.

Have you reached a point in your life where you need to find out who you've grown like, yet you don't know where to start? Sometimes it can be difficult to understand your own behaviour and actions, or why you react in certain situations as you do. It's a very sobering moment when one day you wake up to realizing you don't even know who you're deep within. The path to the inner world is full of great mystery and can often intimidate us, especially when for decades we have been locked out of our own truth. This is where tools and proven systems are becoming useful.

The Enneagram is an ancient system and tool created to help those of us who care to uncover the layers of mass consciousness so that we can dive to discover our true selves. And this book is designed to help make the journey of self-discovery and this ancient tool simpler, easier to understand and faster to use.

13

ORIGINS

*T*he term Enneagram is of Greek origin. Ennea is Greek's number nine, and gram is a drawing. We'd interpret it as a nine-point drawing translated into ordinary English.

In section one of this book, we'll explore in great detail what this drawing looks like and what it means. The critical thing to realize for now is that we're not talking about some new age method to help you cope with life's increasing stresses. There's more to it than meets the eye.

At first, it may seem another one of those entertaining yet juvenile personality tests that have no concrete basis for assuring personal transformation, but if you read through the context of this material and apply proper understanding to it, you will reap the benefits of the contained power.

Some current teachers of this material believe that it's possible to trace variations of the Enneagram symbol to the sacred geometry of Pythagorean mathematicians and mystical mathematicians. While there's a lot of controversy over this theory and who actually originated it, the fact is that it works and is used both in the business world and for spiritual growth. While the Enneagram symbol itself has its roots in ancient times, many individuals have developed the actual system that we use not too long ago today in different ways.

George Gurdijieff, a Russian mystic and teacher is one of those individuals who is credited with the modern reintroduction of the Enneagram symbol. He was a founder of an influential school specialized in' inner work' and his primary way of teaching and using the symbol was through a series of sacred dances or what he called' movements.' He believed in giving his students a direct sense of the meaning of the symbol and the process it represents, but what he did not do was include the ennea-type system as we know it today. We will have to introduce Oscar Ichazo into the story for us to understand who was behind thee system as we know it today.

Oscar Ichazo is credited as the primary individual behind the contemporary Enneagram system. He was a Bolivian man who moved to Peru and later to Buenos Aries in Argentina to study' inner work.' This led to further traveling and searching for wisdom in Asia where he gathered more knowledge across different wisdom traditions that helped him create a systematic way of understanding and applying everything he had learned in his travels. Ichazo combined Taoism, Buddhism, ancient Greek philosophy, Islam, Christianity, and mystical Judaism teachings to form his own school of thought using the ancient Enneagram symbol. Thus from the 1960s, when he began his schooling in Chile, the personality-based Enneagram was offered as a system to help with self-realization and transformation.

The Arica school in Chile, where he taught in the 1960s and early 1970s, was where he first introduced his system of 108 Enneagrams (or Ennneagons, in his terminology). Broadly, these are known as the Passion Enneagram, the Enneagram of the Virtues, the Fixations Enneagram, and the Holy Ideas Enneagram.

During this time in Chile, an American group interested in his work came to South America to study his methods and to experience them firsthand. One of the group's participants was remarkable American psychologist Claudio Naranjo, who recreated his updated version of the personality system of the Enneagram. Although Ichazo and Naranjo began as a teacher and student, each of them went their own way teaching different theories of this Enneagram system and seeing different schools of thought continue to emerge on the subject, don't be surprised to find that some ideas don't always align. Yet, the fundamental goal is not to enter into a debate about who is right or wrong. We are here to develop a healthy understanding of our human psyche. This tool has proven to be very useful to those who practice it and will help you to understand the people around you and yourself better.

Why this matters to you

Understanding why you're acting as you're doing and finding a healthy way to bring out the hidden powers, talents, and aspects of you that would otherwise remain dormant can increase your personal happiness and those of your loved ones. The more you understand why people act as they do, the less likely you're to take things, get discarded or even misunderstand them. There's a greater need for compassion, understanding, and empathy now that we've become more connected than ever as a global community. At work, on social media, at meetings in public, and at home. It helps when human behavior is not such a mystery to you because you can evaluate any given situation and respond rather than react when you have a bearing on the main underlying motives that drive human consciousness.

The bottom line is this.

Anything we can do to know more about ourselves and become better humans is worth diving into and investing a little effort. It takes an open mind and heart, but if you're willing to soak in some new healthy perspectives, I promise to give you insights that can help you.

What This Book Is About

Simply put, this book will answer the big question - Why are you doing what you're doing? It reveals the underlying motives behind each of us, and it will help you to gain clarity on the patterns that do not serve you so that you can improve them as well as shine a light on the positive features that you need to take advantage of.

You will finally discover the real you and become empowered enough to discern the difference between the mask that you wear as a protection. Not only will you learn more about yourself, but with fresh new eyes, you will also begin to see the world understanding why people think, feel, behave and act as they do. This will allow you to detect those that are most compatible with these relationships and to nurture them more. I actually have a chapter that helps you cultivate healthy relationships of love.

I commend you for making this choice to improve yourself and make your fellow human beings better understand. The changes and practices that you integrate as you absorb each chapter will affect your personal success and happiness.

The book is divided into four sections. In section one, we return to the basics so that before integrating this into your life and relationships, you can form a solid foundation. We will dive into the details of the types of Enneagram in section two. In section three, we'll explore more of who you're as well as the Ennea-types subtypes and finally, we'll walk you through integrating this into the most critical areas of your life. You will also have the opportunity to perform an Enneagram test to find out which type and subtype resonates most with you. Now, remember, as is your life, the Enneagram system is a work in progress. Be easy with yourself as you go through this process and try not to get too rigid trying to fit into a particular type or subtype.

The Dark Side of Personality Tests

A woman performed well in her job leading a small team in a major real estate agency until she took one of the most popular personality tests. Her colleagues did not trust her the same way after receiving the results of the personality test. They felt that she didn't have the right personality to be in that position.

In sharing her frustration with me, she said: "Something goes wrong after that day, or I make a mistake that I have this unshakeable feeling that it's because I'm this type of personality and I should be looking for a job that's better suited to that type of personality." This is a real and common problem that many people report once they fall into the downside of relying on shallow personality tests.

The mistake here is fundamental. When we apply rigid labels to ourselves and others that limit the ability to do things outside the test results, it may be like being locked in a small box. I want you to avoid the wrong thinking as we jump into the Enneagram system's basics. You must understand a very simple fact to be able to use this tool effectively.

You're a dynamic, ever-evolving human being. Your experiences, environment, and mindset are changing, and so is your type of personality. This system of nine points is not intended to box you into one category. All nine points are interconnected, and in several types, you can find aspects of you. This is a good thing.

It's possible to be able to find out more about who you truly are and can be done without necessarily fitting into one rigid category. Let's get started.

SECTION I: UNDERSTANDING THE BASICS & BACKGROUND OF THE SYSTEM

14

THE THEORY OF ENNEAGRAM

*I*f we want a better understanding of the Enneagram and how it's meant to help us lead better lives, we must first consider the primary purpose of Ichazo's work. In reality, every person is perfect, fearless and in loving unity with the entire cosmos; there's no conflict within the person between head, heart, and stomach or between the person and others.

"Then something happens: the ego begins to develop, karma accumulates, there's a transition from subjectivity to objectivity; man falls from essence to personality"

It's about enlightening you and prompting you to wake up to a better understanding of your soul and others ' structure. There's a real self and a day-to-day self that forms the individual you know to be together. Usually we operate our entire life from the ordinary self (also known as the ego-self) that we become alienated from that deep true self and that's where all the inner restlessness, confusion and identity crisis emerges from.

Ichazo developed his transformative teachings and methodologies to help us reconcile these two aspects of ourselves and bring back the harmony and wholeness that is ours. The theory is inspired by the Western mystical and philosophical tradition of nine divine forms as discussed by Plato (platonic solids) and then developed in his work-The Enneads-by the Neo-Platonic philosopher Plotinus in the third century.

These are clearly far from new ideas, but what we can conclude is that no one has effectively consolidated all these different schools of thought into a coherent work. His teaching is based on the fact that, as long as an individual remains in pure essence, they are in complete harmony with life and possess the higher essential qualities also known as the Holy Ideas.

Each Holy Idea has a corresponding virtue. As an individual loses awareness and presence, they fall away from that pure Essence and enter the realm of personality where both the Holy Ideas and the Virtues are distorted into ego-fixation and passion, respectively.

Holy Ideas, Virtues, Ego-fixations, and Passions

According to Ichazo's theory, the loss of self-awareness leads to spiritual contraction, which gives way to ego states. In our thoughts, feelings, and actions, we become distorted and disable the connection with the Divine. He's not saying that we shouldn't have passions and ego-fixations, but pointing out that these are lower untamed aspects of ourselves that are actually part of something bigger and better if we're only learning to use them effectively. It becomes our quest to restore that balance and truth in our lives once we recognize that they are distorted versions of pure essence. This is the primary purpose underlying the Enneagram of personality.

The goal is not just to take a test; it's what happens to you once you take the first step of self-analysis through the test.

15

UNDERSTANDING THE MODERN DAY ENNEAGRAM

*N*ow that you have context about the purpose and origin of both the ancient Enneagram symbol and the concept behind it, It's time to turn our attention from the basic history to the actual system so that you can begin to see the value it can bring to your life's development.

When you try to understand and study human behavior, there are different approaches that you can use. Most of them involve the diagnosis of pathological behaviors, and while this is important, it's not a very holistic approach and doesn't consider human behavior in its entirety.

What the Enneagram intends to do is offer a more holistic roadmap and a more precise language to help you understand and express what you're discovering about yourself and others. In order to remain relevant, the detailed typing system needed to grow and factor in the psychological discoveries we have made in the modern world.

It's our job to remember that the purpose of this tool is not to label and categorize others or ourselves into certain fixed states. Instead, it's about opening yourself up to recognize the main behavioral patterns that people tend to fall into, understanding that each individual can exhibit any of these personality traits more dominantly than the other traits depending on their present state of being, environment, and how self-aware they are.

In the interview where Claudio Naranjo explained his role in the tool's creation.

He goes on to say that what Ichazo had was a fundamental map that he then helped to develop to a more advanced level

To better understand the Enneagram tool, we need to consider how the mind works. The mind wants to be strategic about managing and navigating life so that you can survive in the best way. The Enneagram's nine-pointed system is said to be the nine distinct and unique qualities that all human beings possess as special characteristics to help an individual navigate life (including trauma).

Your type of Enneagram is the navigation tool that always secretly influences your behaviour, perceptions, and reactions in ways that you may not always predict. The more you can understand the type of your Enneagram, the more insight you will have about yourself and your usual thinking patterns, because you will recognize that there's one primary way you can perceive and react to things that demonstrate your dominant Enneagram personality. This will enable you to make an informed decision as to whether or not you want to activate other characters that you feel are better suited to the type of person you aspire to be.

It will also help you to better discern between the real self and the self in you. It's a subtle yet complex system, but you don't have to be overwhelmed or confused. As we hit this book's core and uncover this nine-pointed system, take a moment to pause between the description of the type and see which ones are resonating with you. Towards the end of the book, we're going to do a simple Enneagram test to help you figure out where you're standing and which type is your personality most dominant. But let's explore in more detail each numbered point and the Enneagram structure for now.

16

INTRODUCTION TO THE DIFFERENT ENNEAGRAM TYPES

*B*ased on the personality system's Enneagram teachings, we know there are nine points. Each of them has a unique name of type.

1. *The Perfectionist also called the Reformer.*

2. *The Giver also called the Helper.*

3. *The Achiever also called the Performer.*

4. *The Romantic also called the Individualist.*

5. *The Observer also called the Investigator.*

6. *The Loyalist also called the Doubter.*

7. *The Enthusiast also called the Dreamer.*

8. The Challenger also called the Leader.

9. The Peacemaker also called the Diplomat.

However, it's worth mentioning that the system contains more than just these nine types. There are also centers and wings that play a major role in interpreting and understanding your results when taking the test.

Centers:

Centers further arrange the nine points into three groups. On the diagram they form a triad. Classifying the numbered points as the Instinctive Center for Type 1, 8 and 9; the Feeling Center for Type 2, 3 and 4; and finally the Thinking Center for Personality Type 5, 6 and 7.

The Wings:

The wings are what help us to recognize the fact that we are all connected irrespective of type and also that we are not stuck exclusively and rigidly to a numbered point. As a matter of fact, unless we embrace and develop "our wings," it will still be hard to reach our full potential in life.

We dive more into the centers and wings in the next chapter, where you can even get a visual sense of the Enneagram to help you better connect with the system.

As you can see, there are added layers of complexities that can be very intriguing to an individual who is interested. As complicated as this system may seem, it's very dynamic and simple as soon as you understand and connect to the diagram structure itself, because it will give your mind a working mental image from which to grasp more about your natural proclivities.

When you try to find out more about yourself, others and why you're acting as you do, the Internet has a lot of solutions to choose from. Unfortunately, most of them don't have the merit to give you a response that can transform your life. However, the Enneagram personality tool is one of the few globally recognized systems that not only helps you to learn more about your personality, but also expands your awareness to show you how to tap into realms that go far beyond superficial trends. Best of all, it gives you insights into how your personality type will behave when you're exposed to unhealthy, stressful situations and how good things can be when you're on the healthy path of personality development.

17

STRUCTURE OF THE DIAGRAM

The structure of the conventional Enneagram diagram is designed to help you connect visually, mentally and emotionally with the tool. I bet you're wondering why the system is numerically numbered 1-9 before we start dissecting it. I was also curious about that. Does a higher numerical ranking mean that there's more value in one personality type compared to another?

Absolutely not! There's no value difference between the larger number and the smaller number. So just because someone is an eight doesn't mean they're better than a three.

. . .

I firmly believe no one is better or worse than the other. With different attributes that can be expressed in healthy or unhealthy ways, each character is unique. Certainly, you'll find some people who want a specific number because it's better to be that type of personality according to society, but I just don't agree with that notion. I think that if underdeveloped, any symbol can become a handicap. The key is to nurture the healthy aspects that most resonate with whichever you type. Don't get so upset about what the best personality is "people say." The best character for you is to be authentically yourself and appear as the highest version you can be.

Starting from the outside layers and working your way in is the fastest way to understand the diagram. Imagine a circle drawing. Then inside the circle a triangle and let it touch all three corners. Mark the three points of the triangle 9, 3 and 6 in clockwise position with 9 sitting at the top of the circle.

All you have to do now is make six points equidistant from the circumference of the circle and specify the remaining numbers 1,2,4,5,7 and 8 to fill the gaps. Be sure to do it in a clockwise motion and symmetrically. Each of these numbers is one of the top nine types of personality. If you do this activity by hand, you will begin to notice that internal lines can connect the nine points in some way and that points 3, 6 and 9 actually form an equilateral triangle. You can connect the remaining six points as shown in the diagram below. The importance of these inner lines leads us to another vital lesson when it comes to an understanding of the Enneagram tool.

THE PEACEMAKER
9
THE CHALLENGER 8   1 THE REFORMER
THE ENTHUSIAST 7   2 THE GIVER
THE LOYALIST 6   3 THE ACHIEVER
THE OBSERVER 5   4 THE ROMANTIC

The tool is used to help a person identify their most dominant type within the nine-point system at a fundamental level. There's more to it, though, than those who want to dive deeper. Between the nine points there's also interconnection. So while you may find that your basic personality is a 2, discovering a little more of yourself in all nine types is not uncommon. This is where the Centers and Wings come into play.

All Enneagram teachers and authors agree that we are all born with a specific dominant type of personality that emerges in childhood to help us adapt to our environment.

As infants, we don't really have a developed sense of ourselves. The ego hasn't yet been activated and just spend some time in a park if you're unclear about this. Notice how the small child has no sense of identity in a pram. They can hardly tell the difference between their fingers and their toes or whether or not a doll belongs to them. Then look at the infants who are beginning to become more self-conscious. They can identify their parents and siblings, but they still have no sense of themselves. Then we observe five-year-olds, chasing a ball around. The ball owner knows that it belongs to her, and if you grab it from her, she would probably cry, but the self is still very fluid. Once they reach the age of seven and older, the self is well defined, and it's all about taking ownership and determining "me" and "mine." We developed a sense of self in order to help us fit into this world and survive, depending on our environment, what our caregivers taught us, how they treated us and what we were exposed to.

Therefore, we may generalize that our formative years and everything we have been exposed to help shape our personalities. We learned to rely more heavily on the type of personality that would enable us in the world around us to survive and feel safe. Some of what we ended up choosing may be wonderful, but maybe some aspects are not at all healthy yet we still appear as that person in the world. In addition, we may have neglected to develop and leverage the influences of the connected qualities and special capabilities that we may possess. That's why it can be worthwhile to get to know what center you belong to and what wings you have. Let's discuss further the role of the three centers and the wings before jumping into each of the next section's nine points.

Centers:

As mentioned above, Centers are segmented into a

triad. These are intelligence centers that will fall into each of the numbered points. Each center will have three types of personality. The triad consists of the center of thought, the center of feeling, and the center of gut.

Also known as the centers of head, heart, and gut. These centers are deliberately designed and designated for the specific areas on the diagram. Centers are usually differentiated from one another based on how the person usually interprets life and others.

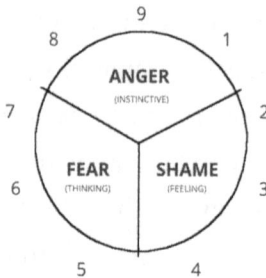

Thinking Center:

. . .

Head types are usually too stuck in their heads. They tend to pull out of relationships. The head center is a cognitive center and the people in this triad love thinking, analyzing, and cautiously approaching things. Picture you've been at a party for a moment. If you're part of the center of thought, then your natural tendency and preference would be at or near the door so that you can have a better view and just observe others.

Some authors like to refer to them as mental-based types. Their dominant emotion to keep in check is Fear.

The Feeling Center:

The types of heart are usually people engaging in relationships and continually looking for others. They are very concerned with other people's feelings and interactions. Go back to the scene of the party. Instead of standing by the door this time to see who's present and what's happening around you, you'd be the first to mingle, introduce yourself to people, and try to connect with as many people as possible.

. . .

Some people will refer to these types as feeling-based. Their dominant emotion is Shame.

The Instinctive Center:

The types of gut are instinctual. They are very straightforward and have no fear of being confrontational. People tend to act first in this triad and then think and feel later. If we take the last example of this party, you would know if this triad would fit your perfect approach from the moment you entered the room. Are you, in your interaction with others, bold, loud, hearty and jovial? Maybe you're coming off too hard that others often find offensive or intimidating. And if your type of person is not shy when it comes to offering constructive criticism even if it's to the party's host, then I would say this is your center.

Some authors will refer to these types as types based on the body. Anger is the dominant emotion to keep in check here.

. . .

According to the Enneagram Institute, each type is the result of a specific relationship with a cluster of issues that characterize that center. Most simply, these issues are about a powerful, mostly unconscious, emotional response to the loss of self-contact.

In other words, you have a particular unconscious emotional response that often surfaces as a result of the loss of contact between the little self of everyday life and the true self. The three centers that have been grouped into Thinking, Instinctive and Feeling centers have as their dominant emotions Fear, Anger and Shame respectively.

So if you take the Enneagram test and discover that you're a type 6 and after a little reflection you realize that fear is one of the greatest paralyzers that holds you back from greatness, then you have just confirmed that you're dominant in that. So when you're improving your life and working hard to manifest a life you love, it's important to keep a close watch on fear because that would be your biggest saboter.

. . .

Each intelligence center has certain liabilities and assets that are included in it that will possess the assigned types of personality that come under that group. Type three, for example, falls into the "feeling center," suggesting that their most dominant unconscious emotion is shameful. It also means that they have certain strengths and qualities in relation to "feelings," which is why they fall into that triad.

Just so we're clear, that doesn't mean you're not going to experience other emotions. Think of the group in which you're as having a theme. Whatever your theme is, that will be your most dominant emotion to deal with.

•

The Wings:

The reason that I believe wings are an important aspect to be included in your interpretation of the results of your Enneagram is that in truth, none of us can be fully summarized by a single personality type.

We are unique and complex people. Always evolving

and changing from moment to moment. Our character has to be a combination of different qualities as well. The wings help to integrate this concept into the system.

Although some Enneagram teachers argue that we have only one wing, I am convinced that we need more than one wing. The number 1 is connected to 2 on one side and 9 on the other, even if we judge it from a strictly numerical point of view. The type that is adjacent to the 1 is what we call your wing. Just as you need both wings for a bird or plane to fly, you need wings to soar. These wings compliment your core personality. They connect you to your "closest neighbors," giving you access to various resources and features that can be very useful.

Are both wings equally dominant and do you need to develop each individually?

Yes...and no. It's not an easy question to answer in fact. The Institute of the Enneagram provides some insight into this. "People's observation leads us to conclude that while the two-wing theory applies to some individuals, most people have a dominant one. In the vast majority of people, while the so-called second wing is always operational to some degree, the dominant wing is much more important."

I think the most important thing to remember when it comes to your wings is that you will resonate more with one si. As years go by, this may also change, and you may find yourself switching and displaying more of the less influential wing's qualities. Either way, it's good to be aware of both and figure out which one aligns best with your basic personality and the human being you want to become.

An effective way to approach and understand your wings:

I walked into my favorite frozen yogurt parlor not too long ago to take a break from the hour-long shopping trip I had just finished. Unfortunately, this refreshing break I wasn't the only one I needed. It'd be waiting in line for about 5 minutes before I finally got my turn. Instead of scowling and feeling sorry for myself, I decided to observe with what the people before me were ordering. When I realized how unique we are all, it was a rather exciting experience.

Some people wanted no toppings at all but the plain base. Others wanted four different toppings.

An adolescent girl just before me wanted to know if she could get six different toppings! I thought it was a bit too much. I felt quite modest by the time it was my turn when I asked for a frozen yogurt of medium size with just Nutella as the topping! Yes, I'm a junkie for Nutella, what can I tell you?

This is the point of the story...

As we all differ uniquely within our preferences and the relationships with our wings will also vary from individual to individual. The wings are not the frozen yogurt; they are the toppings with which you can choose to flavor your yogurt (type of core personality). We all have access to our two wings, and sometimes one will lean more heavily towards one, or another.

The more you know your preference, the easier it will be to use your wings. Some people absolutely don't like any topping. We'd call them a light wing in this case; some want lots of toppings or too much of one kind. Those we could call strong wings. Others like me want the right amount of toppings, and we can call it balanced double wings. Connecting to your wings can help you to understand the subtleties of your core personality type, regardless of your preference.

As you lean more to one side or the other in your wings, you will expand your perspective and increase your ability to handle tension, creating a greater potential for reframing influencers that no longer serve you. Each core personality type on each side of the nine-point system comes with a connected "close neighbor." In the next section, some of the gifts and challenges that each wing carries will be explored as we unlock the qualities of core personality types. Let's get to it.

SECTION II: TYPES OF ENNEAGRAM PERSONALITIES IN DETAIL

18

TYPE ONE ENNEAGRAM OF PERSONALITY TYPES

*T*ype One: The Perfectionist, also called the Reformer

Type One's are usually considered. They enjoy a feeling of control and is constantly in need of doing what's best. Some of the core values are integrity and responsibility for this type.

It's critical for those who fall into this first type to be considered a good person, often taking a black and white approach to everything. Something is good or bad

Famous celebrities like Hilary Clinton, Martha Stewart or even world reformers like Nelson Mandela are likely to fall into this type.

Typical qualities are attributed to some. Character

traits such as purposeful, principled, self-controlled, integrity-filled and pragmatic.

They may be quite calm and serene, but they are also known to be highly critical of themselves and others. They tend to be very judgmental and uncompromising. Since they fall into the Instinctive Center, rage and anger are common experiences, but they do a good job of suppressing it because they don't really like expressing emotions.

If you're a type one person, you're more likely to be interested in doing the right thing at all times. Common sense is what you believe in, and you're often very responsible for wondering what's wrong with people who don't take life seriously and take responsibility for themselves. You have high standards and you tend to be an idealist doing the best you can to improve the world around you, hence the common term "reformer." You're detail-oriented, accurate in your way of communication, and grounded.

How to improve yourself:

The best way to help your personal growth is to practice being less critical of yourself if you resonate most with type one. Learn to release healthy anger, rage, resentment, or anything else.

It will also be a liberating experience to learn to forgive yourself and others for errors, as it will better empower you to deal with the imperfections you're aware of. Also, allow yourself to have fun!

Your Wings

The Nine Wing:

*Gifts:*Some of the gifts this wing brings to the strict perfectionist include, but are not limited to the following.

- That strong urge you often have to correct or improve people and things are significantly reduced.
- You can have more points of view and be more open and collaborative.
- There is an increased sense of relaxation, confidence and acceptance.

Type Two: The Giver also called the Helper

This type of person is naturally very empathetic, caring and helpful to others, hence the term "helper."

Think of an iconic figure like Diana-Princess of Wales or Mother Teresa and you have a good understanding of this type of personality. If we dared to go too far, we might even assign this numbered point to religious archetypes like Jesus Christ.

Some qualities are attributed to the twos type. Character traits like authenticity, compassion, generosity, possessiveness, and caring.

Because they have such a strong need for love, they can often become pleasant to people.

Type twos have deep-rooted values that focus on their relationships and puts a lot of energy into them, to the extent that they can sometimes neglect their personal needs. Undoubtedly Empaths would be considered to fall into this category. They are grouped as part of the Feeling Center, being a feeling-based type, and this unfortunately leads to the dominant sense of shame.

Often a person in this category will try to mask the shame they're experiencing and that feeling of not being good enough by overcompensating their interactions with others so that people can think of them as good.

If you're a type two personality, then you're more likely to be an emotional sponge that's always experiencing more than others, which makes you really good at supporting and giving. But you may have realized that it's a bit tricky to give yourself or take time to meet your needs. On autopilot, you need to be careful not to absorb emotions, as this will destabilize your sense of being grounded. You're a caring, communicative and naturally generous person, but you have to make sure that it doesn't happen from a place of dependence.

How to improve yourself:

Make self-care and self-love a priority in your life. Train yourself to take care of your own needs. I know saying no and setting boundaries is difficult but you have to start recognizing when to set boundaries for your own mental, emotional, spiritual and physical protection.

Your Wings

The One Wing:

*Gifts:*Some of the gifts this wing brings to the helpful type of giver include but are not limited to the following.

- You may feel more influenced by being more generous and not just giving. It helps you to realize that you don't have to do everything on your own.

*Challenges:*Some of the challenges this wing brings to the helpful type of giver include but are not limited to the following.

- As you become more involved with work and less involved with your inner self, you may end up neglecting your needs and becoming a workaholic. Hence the danger of excessive pride as the reason for your work.

Type Three: The Achiever also referred to as the Performer

An achiever, commonly referred to as the performer, is the term given to type three personalities. While some similarities exist between type one and three, a person in this category is driven more by success and the best in life. They wants to be admired and validated.

Type threes are hard-working, diligent, and some-times even somewhat obsessive, which is excellent because it keeps them going until they achieve their objectives. Being the best is something that really cares about this type of personality, and that's why they often become the top performers in their chosen industry. Individuals such as Muhammad Ali, Will Smith, Tom Cruise, Elon Musk, and Oprah Winfrey would undoubtedly be classified as achievers in our modern world.

The qualities this person possesses can be outstanding, and it can also be quite harmful if they focus on the wrong thing. The desire to be the best at work, look good, demonstrate success and always win can make a Type Three super competitive, tense and may even lead them to step over others just to get ahead.

Certain qualities are attributed to this Type Three such as: being driven, self-confident, image-conscious, adaptable, focused, determined, excellent, energetic and great in leadership and communication. This type of personality loves to look good and is usually a smart and wonderful person to learn from when you want to excel in life as well. They have a lot of energy and enthusiasm for life that many find contagious, and this really helps them as they raise up the ranks in life or become self-made successes.

They too fall into the Thinking Center, meaning that shame is an underlying emotional theme that they have to deal with on an ongoing basis. Because the three are so focused on image and outward success, it's usually difficult for him or her to know how to handle emotions, particularly shame. For type threes, denial is often the preferred option.

Their coping mechanism for shame strives to become what they believe to be the most valuable and successful individual they can possibly be, in the hope that this will dissolve that underlying restlessness and feelings of shame and inadequacy.

If you're a type three personality then productivity, high performance and excellence move the needle for you. You love to be the best and to be recognized for it. Forward momentum, you're naturally motivated and motivated to succeed by others around you. There's no doubt about it, you think differently, you dream bigger than most people, and you're trying to achieve more than most people. Your energy is often contagious, and people usually love to be around you because you fire them up.

How to improve yourself:

Take some time to regularly audit yourself and acquire clarity about what true success and happiness mean to you. Looking inside may be a bit frightening, but this is where your real power lies.

Material success must not be confused with fulfillment and self-worth, and you must draw your power from the real Source of Life, not from the power of the agency. Titles, awards and external validation can not be your true value. And that deep sense of meaning that you long for in your life will not come from accomplishments, which is why taking the time to go inside and find out who you really are will enable you to emerge better and more prosperous in every conceivableway.

Your Wings

The Two Wings:

*Gifts:*Some of the gifts this wing brings to the achievement type include, but are not limited to, the following: It allows you to appreciate people and the contribution they make in your life.

- You also become more aware of your needs and see the value of prioritizing non-work relationships.

*Challenges:*Some of the challenges this wing brings to the competitive achievement include but are not limited to the following.

- You may experience much more disappointment and self-criticism if your accomplishments are successful. Pleasant people may take a toll on your actions.

The Four Wing:

*Gifts:*Some of the gifts this wing brings to the competitive attainder include but are not limited to the following.

- One of the best gifts you will receive from this wing is the realization that self-development and time to understand the inner world has tremendous value.

Type Four: The Romantic also called the Individualist

A type four person is mostly referred to as the individualist, but I also like the term romantic.

This person is super creative, he sees beauty and magnificence in everything and tends to romanticize things. Think of famous people like Oscar Wilde, Michael Jackson, William Shakespeare, or the Persian poet Hafiz, and you now have a better idea of people who would fall into this type.

Character qualities associated with this type of

personality include creativity, authenticity, courage, passion, and emotional depth.

However, they can also considered very temperamental, self-absorbed, and dramatic. Type fours have an underlying sense of melancholy because they invariably feel like something is missing.

Fours are long to be understood and treasured for who they really are, but they regularly feel misunderstood and disappointed. Such a person will create an inner mental landscape where he feels more liberating and nourishing as a way to escape from the harsh, cruel world that never "gets them" them or their sensitivities.

It has been said that the majority of fours are artistic or very much artistic as a means of self-expression, but whether this is the case or not, a type four personality will tend to experience a great deal of disappointment and dissatisfaction in the world as they feel different and unique from those who are not like them. And in some idealistic way they will try to find and express wholeness and beauty.

Being the most emotional of all types of personality, they tend to struggle the most with the dominant emotional theme of shame. They are part of the

Feeling Center and undoubtedly "feel" deeply, so their discomfort is likely to be more pronounced and easier to spot. However, they try to mask this by focusing on how unique and special they are, even though it may lead to rollercoaster experiences plunging into deep depression and other negative emotions to the other extreme of beauty, joy, fantasy, and inspired creativity.

If you're a type four personality, then you value individualism and self-expression. You love to see someone sharing their feelings authentically, yet you notice that sometimes you can be really warm and welcoming, while at other times you can get people dry and almost cold. You can be ecstatic one day and plunge into depression soon after. Envy and jealousy often rage on you even though you don't even like to admit it to yourself.

How to improve yourself:

That inner critic, often so loud, needs to be tamed and put on silent. Internalizing blame is very unhealthy for you and requires a shift in your perception and how negative emotions and situations are processed.

Learn to openly speak your truth without losing your emotional control. Find a way to balance your emotional rollercoaster so you can stop falling into the pit of despair and depression.

Your Wings

The Two Wings:

*Gifts:*Some of the gifts this wing brings to the creative, intense individualist type include but are not limited to the following.

- The desire to be successful and look good that comes organically from this wing actually helps you to be real. In short, you're more capable of balancing your inner and outer world.

Challenges:

Some of the challenges this wing brings to the creative, intense individualistic type include, but are not limited to, the following.

- There is a tendency to want to fix others and the outer world instead of yourself.
- You're more likely to be agitated and depressed as the ongoing performance pressure builds throughout your life.

Type Five: The Observer also called the Investigator

The Observer personality, commonly referred to as the Investigator is usually brilliant, highly intellectual, keen on learning on an ongoing basis, and is most comfortable in the realm of thinking. This type of person tends to be very independent, enjoying loneliness. They enjoy gathering information and observing patterns all around them trying to make sense of their world and environment. Individuals such as Albert Einstein, Nikola Tesla, Isaac Newton, and Marie Curie are just a few examples of such people.

Some of the qualities associated with type fives are innovative, self-reliant, isolated, secret, curious, perceptive, scholarly, quiet and reserved. They are intense, intelligent thinkers and take great pleasure in tending to their mind's affairs rather than trying to fit into the world.

As mental-based types, fives will often detach themselves from relationships, and many will consider them to be emotionally inexpressive. But they're not all. Some fives care about family and relationships, but it takes a lot of time to recreate and pursue their passions alone. It's not easy to figure out what's going on under a five's surface level and they have an exaggerated need for privacy.

Type five personality falls into the' Thinking Center ' group making fear one of the dominant negative themes they have to deal with. Fear of inadequacy is one of the great battles that must be overcome when dealing with the outside world because they feel unable to actively handle the outside world. Maybe that's why they tend to be detached and their own feelings from others.

Expert says that fives like to leave the open world because of their unconscious fear and belief that they can better relate to it by going into their minds and using it to penetrate the nature of our society. Unfortunately, that usually doesn't work too well for them and in their fear of being overwhelmed by people or emotions they may find arrogant and dismissive.

If you're a type five, then you're likely to value knowledge and continuing education a lot, especially in the topics you're interested in. Some people think you're too intellectual and you may be quite literal at times, but you don't really care.

Small talk and gossip are annoying you and you prefer isolation. You tend to get stuck in your head and prefer to hang out with people who give you plenty of room to think about things. You like to be thorough in everything you do, and you enjoy deep, meaningful conversations very much. In fact, you can talk about it in great technical details for a very long time when you're passionate about something. Reconnecting with your body and heart's sensations and energy is a task even though you know it's good for you and, above all, personal freedom and autonomy bring you great pleasure.

How to improve yourself:

Start by increasing the amount of time you spend reconnecting with your body and emotions. Your ability to gain access to your energy and higher perceptions of the spirit will only strengthen you.

Create for yourself a safe environment where you can regularly embark on this quest so that you can combine your intellectual strength with your spiritual strength.

Put a little more effort into the relationships you care about.

Let your loved ones know you care about them and be more expressive of your feelings, even if you feel a little uncomfortable about them. Let yourself feel emotions like happiness, being in love, gratitude, affection, etc. This will open a channel for others to pour the same into your life and help you deal with the feelings of loneliness and inadequacy that sometimes resurface.

Your Wings

The Two Wings:

*Gifts:*Some of the gifts this wing brings to the quiet expert type include but are not limited to the following.

- You will have the unusual ability to connect your river for a type five personality.

Type Six: The Doubter also referred to as the Loyal Skeptic

A type six personality is always alert and conscious of their environment and responsibilities. Knowing the rules and protecting those who are under their care is extremely important to sixes. They are very trustworthy and the people they care about value being there. Unfortunately, between trusting and distrusting others, they tend to feel conflicted. They often bounce with a tendency to doubt themselves and question others between skepticism and certainty.

They are very sober-minded people and take problem-solving rather seriously to the point where it becomes a burden on them. For a six, worry and anxiety are common emotions. In this type, peace of mind is always lacking, and they usually struggle with a profound sense of insecurity. If you want an idea of celebrities that could be classified as type six individuals, think of Ellen DeGeneres, Tom Hanks, and Richard Nixon.

Some of the character qualities associated with type six include trustworthy, responsible, committed, loyal, and trustworthy.

The six also fall into the' Thinking Center ' making fear (which often turns out to be worried and anxious) the more dominant emotions.

Stress levels for a six are always high and worry seems to be a constant companion as their life outlook is often quite negative. They will focus more on the negatives than on the positive ones of any given situation.

If you're a type six, then you tend to pay close attention to people and issues. You're really good at anticipating issues and creating solutions, and in others you tend not to like ambiguity. But you may have realized that you could become very pessimistic, doubtful, and even project on other people some of your fears. Sometimes you like playing the Devil's advocate. As you grow, it becomes more important to overcome the disconnect between the mind and the body, and even if you're cautious (maybe even phobic), you're also showing a lot of courage as you try to move forward even when fear holds on to you.

How to improve yourself:

Find ways to deal with the crippling effects of fear in your life and get better at directly addressing it. Ask an expert or trusted friend for some help and support.

Learn to take things with a light heart.

Reconnect more with your body and feelings and create a safe space to do so in order to relax your mental processes and help in this new experiment. The more comfortable and safe you feel mentally, the faster and more enjoyable the mental-body connection will become.

Your Wings

The Five Wing:

*Gifts:*Some of the gifts this wing brings to the loyal

skeptic type include but are not limited to the following.

- This wing helps you make more reasonable and sound decisions. It also makes you open-minded and able to take multiple perspectives.
- You will also experience a deeper sense of inner trust and self-confidence as an observer and authority on your focused interest. This helps to eradicate the need to seek validation from others.

Challenges:

Some of the challenges this wing brings to the loyal skeptic type include but are not limited to the following.

- This wing may amplify your fears and anxiety or any sense of inadequacy that you may have.
- You may notice a tendency to be too stuck in your head and not aligned enough with your feelings. You begin to see more good and become less inclined to imagine the worst of people and the world at large.
- You may notice a shift inside and outside of

how you approach others, how playful, lighthearted and enthusiastic you feel. It's even possible to realize and even laugh at your own fears as you see them.

Challenges:

Some of the challenges this wing brings to the loyal skeptic type include but are not limited to the following.

- This wing will amplify the common tendency to fear and avoid pain at all costs. This may lead you to seek all sorts of unhealthy distractions or to withdraw even more from life.
- Instead, you may start to avoid confronting issues that require your attention and seek escapism.

Type Seven: The Dreamer also called the Enthusiast

The dreamer is spontaneous, a real pleasure seeker and loves to live life to the maximum.

Having fun is the top priority of this type of personality and they always seek to catch the next exciting adventure just around the corner. Also known as enthusiasts or epicures, seven are mental-based types that are forward-thinking and can't be limited to just one thing. They believe in unlimited opportunities, and it demonstrates their variety of passions and interests. Think about people such as Steve Jobs, Robert Downey Jr., George Clooney, and Elton John. We believe they would definitely fall into this type of personality.

Some of the primary qualities attributed to those in this type of personality include enthusiasm, spontaneity, resourcefulness, adventure, optimistic fun and exciting.

Some seven are extroverts though not all of them are great communicators in general. Unfortunately, being mental-based types, they are part of the' Thinking Center' which makes the dominant emotional theme of fear their greatest hurdle to overcome. And it appears in the form of avoiding pain for a seven.

As a seeker of pleasure, a seven will do anything to prevent pain and sometimes seek distractions that turn into overindulgence. But in order to avoid suffering, they rationalize and justify this downward tendency. Also, as they shift so frequently into the next big thing, sevens tend to be very scattered, making it difficult for them to dive deeply into any single idea, or stay the course in relationships and at work. True devotion is hard for a seven because they are such believers in "the next big thing" that makes it hard to narrow down their vision and concentrate wholeheartedly on one thing.

They are usually known as "big talkers" and prone to addiction and over-stimulation, which can be in the form of substance use, gambling, shopping, adventure seeking. It's easy for you to multi-task and you hate the feeling of constriction.

Everything you do has to be fun because it's who you're. You're definitely a multi-passionate human being, so the commonly preached idea of finding your "one thing" is meaningless to you. You love learning new things and with an optimism that others truly admire approach life.

Yet you don't really care about "saving face" or getting people impressed. You just care to do your own thing while at it and have an epic time. You can bounce back very quickly from negative emotions and situations. But deep down, you've come to realize you can't stand the pain experience and it scares you. Negative states of mind, depression, and suffering are unbearable whether they are your own or others. Introspection is not something you enjoy, and you go through cycles of anxiety and desperation that drive you to seek remedies at any cost.

How to improve yourself:

Create a secure support structure that allows you to cope with your pain, loss, deprivation or any other suffering you have avoided. Learn to embrace your inner world and reconnect with it.

Be more present at the moment and find peace of mind and comfort without using stimulants. It won't be easy, I'm not saying it will be, but you can do it.

With your level of intelligence, resourcefulness, creativity, natural strength and optimism you can gain true freedom and enjoy being the expanding, adventurous human you were meant to be while remaining grounded in your true self.

Your Wings

The Six Wing:

*Gifts:*Some of the gifts this wing brings to the enthusiast include but are not limited to the following. It creates a sense of seriousness and motivates your desire for unlimited freedom.

Challenges:

Some of the challenges this wing might bring to the enthusiast include, but are not limited to, the following.

- That increased sense of duty might potentially begin to feel like a burden.
- Your underlying fears may appear to be amplified, self-doubt may increase, and you may end up feeling guilty. If your selfish desires combine with a need for immediate satisfaction, then in the name of pleasure and gain you might run the risk of going too far. Even if it means making the most of others to get what you want.
- You may become more self-absorbed and look down on others and treat them with a sense of superiority.

Type Eight: The Challenger also called the Leader

The best statement to summarize this type of personality is *"I am a master of my fate. I am the captain of my soul."* Indeed, this type of personality believes in taking full control of their lives and being perceived as the powerful, active leader and protector. Justice, fairness, and independence for type eight are of great value. They will fight back with vengeance if wrong.

Eights are body-based types that give them strong physical appetites and strong instincts. They are bold, they are active in making decisions, they love to be independent and they are very intense people. A person typed as an eight generally desires a great life, and They is ready to go out and fight for that desire. In our modern world, individuals such as Donald Trump embody this type.

Some of the qualities attributed to type eights include self-confidence, courage, willingness, determination, power, courage, generosity, and domination.

Eights can sometimes be difficult to handle, especially if their personalities have been developed in unhealthy ways. They are predisposed to make their emotional theme anger in the 'Instinctive Center'. Type Eights really know how to get angry. Whenever they don't get their own way, or things go wrong, they're very quick to anger, and that anger can quickly turn into rage and physical violence if it remains unchecked.

They produce a lot of energy to meet challenges with the right mental and physical attitude. A feeling of weakness is the one thing an eight can't stand. Vulnerability (based on how it's defined by society) is also something that a type eight would keep clear of, making it difficult to have a deep and intimate relationship with the type eight.

They still need to feel in control and powerful even in their intimate relationships. Eight are fierce when it comes to protecting their family, friends, and their caregivers. They're going to go to the ends of the earth and do whatever it takes to accomplish the mission.

If you're a type eight personality, you've noticed a tendency to be excessive within you. Some people call you bossy even if you don't get the reason. You see it as being firm, focused, clear, assertive, and leading to victory for others.

Idleness, weakness, shyness are all things that you can not stand in yourself and others, and you prefer when people address you directly and confidently. You may get outraged when provoked, and you tend to be vengeful towards people. But you keep an open mind.

How to improve yourself:

you have a lot of energy. Probably the most energetic of all the nine types, which means that you need to constructively direct that energy. Incorporate some self-control into your life and do not allow your automatic reaction to remain anger and aggression just because it's a comfortable habit.

Redefine your meaning of vulnerability and learn to receive love and affection. Request help from someone you trust or hire an expert if you need some personal assistance and support. It's not a kind of weakness. Don't get caught up in this false belief. Improving yourself is a form of strength and empowers you to become a better leader and protector.

Your Wings

The Seven Wings:

*Gifts:*Some of the gifts this wing brings to the active controller include but are not limited to the following.

- Tapping into this wing's gifts will calm you down, increase your happiness and help you move more enthusiastically through life. It gives you a light heart and dissolves some of that ruthlessness that often rules your life.

- Instead of being a lone wolf trying to make it all yourself, you'll start to value connecting with other people, exchanging ideas, expressing your thoughts and acting out your fantasies in a more harmonious way.

Type Nine: The Peacemaker also called the Diplomat

A Type Nine is generally known as someone that "goes with the flow" in life. Above all, they value harmony, peace and balance and do whatever they can to avoid conflict and rivalry. Individuals like the Dalai Lama, Queen Elizabeth II, Abraham Lincoln, and Grace Kelly are all great examples of people of this type of personality.

Some of the essential qualities associated with this type of personality include tolerance, robustness, reliability, soundness, calmness, and goodwill.

Nines are body-based types that love to get along

with everyone and are pretty awesome to be around. Nines can tolerate a lot and usually approach every situation in an optimistic manner. They like seeing the best in others and have a strong belief that things are always going to work for the best. They believe in a friendly universe and want to have as much as possible an open mind and heart.

They are grouped in the 'Instinctive Center' to watch out for their dominant emotional theme. All this calmness, if left unchecked, can turn into something dark and unhealthy. And it happens mostly in the form of emotions suppressed and denied.

Because of the inherent desire to be a peace-maker in the world, nines generally deny the threatening emotions of anger that arise so frequently. With their instinctual drives and dominant emotions in this area, they are the most out of touch with these baser emotions. Their need to avoid conflict at all costs (including internal conflict) causes their unpleasant hidden feelings to become repressed. A nine is also prone to inaction and procrastination, particularly when They senses unpleasant emotions.

· · ·

If you're a type nine personality, then you value the profound connection with the world and those you care about. You tend to change in a conservative way and sometimes struggle with a lack of motivation. Being out in nature gives you the most satisfying feeling

People think you're warm, nurturing, reliable and attentive. This self-sacrificing tendency, however, carries some significant disadvantages that you don't like to face up to as it causes discomfort. You may notice that people are beginning to take you for granted or undervalue everything you're doing for them, and it can be very discouraging. You have a tendency to "forget yourself" as you easily merge with others that make it really hard for you to create personal boundaries.

How to improve yourself:

Call yourself to take more risks in life. Create a safe space in your life where you can train yourself to integrate harmony and conflict so you can stop avoiding them all the time.

. . .

Pay more attention to your own needs and learn to set clear boundaries. Reconnect with your emotions and embrace conflict or anger discomfort as it appears within you so that you can deal with it boldly. Instead of suppressing the negative emotions that appear. Give yourself time and space to process all your feelings.

With your top priorities, be more structured and strategic. If it's a matter of getting more organized then ask for help or acquire one of the many modern tools to help you better prioritize activities on a daily basis.

Your Wings

The Eight Wing:

*Gifts:*Some of the gifts this wing brings to the adaptive peacemaker include but are not limited to the following.

- The positive influence this wing has on your core personality as a peacemaker. It will help you build some structure around your life and activities. You will develop a more focused perspective and lead a principle-based life.
- Instead of accepting dysfunction as the standard way of life, you will feel empowered to be more actively involved in changing things that go wrong. You will be more action-oriented, but it will come from a place of purpose and certainty.

Challenges:

Some of the challenges this wing brings to the adaptive peacemaker include but are not limited to the following:

- The increased need to do what is right and make the world perfect may lead to even more procrastination and distraction. The fear of not getting it right may actually become a huge obstacle.

- You may be caught in the trap of doing what you "should do" or what you're expected to do rather than what you really want to do.

SECTION III: INSTINCTS, SUBTYPES AND VARIANTS WITHIN THE ENNEAGRAM OF PERSONALITY TOOL

19

DIVING DEEPER INTO WHO YOU REALLY ARE

$\mathcal{L}$ike animals, we as humans have continued to evolve has physical and conative beings. Our evolution has required us to develop strategies that will allow us to survive and extend our species' life on this planet. What the Enneagram does, is facilitate a better understanding of the instinctual strategies that we have developed as human beings, and shows us how it affects a person's behaviour in different ways. This is more than just getting to know your personality type; it's about pulling back the curtain of the influences that drive you to act as you do.

There are three basic human instincts that the Enneagram teachers, and out of these three we see a detailed dissection of how these instincts interact and combine with the nine types of personality. These are:

- Instinct for self-preservation.
- Social Instinct.
- Sexual Instinct.

All three instincts are within us and often ruling unconsciously behind our life strategies. While these three are always present, one tends to dominate more, and we tend to prioritize and develop that particular drive while the other tends to be less dominant. And because we don't make improving the least dominant one a priority, it tends to become our blind spot.

Think of these three instincts as you'd be a layered cake. At the top we have our most controlling one, in the middle we have the second one that supports the predominant one, and at the bottom we have the least developed instinct.

· · ·

Again, even here we find some conflict with some schools stating that they should not be referred to as subtypes, while others teach that they are actually subtypes of the nine-point system. Anyway, we don't care about the label. We're only concerned with how we can better understand who we are and why we're acting as we do. The primary instinct with which we identify in combination with our personality type of Enneagram helps shape our life path and the choices we make.

Since that is our core focus, after a brief under-standing of what each instinct entails, we will dive into each of the twenty-seven combinations.

Instinct for self-preservation:

The need to preserve our body and its life force. Keep away from threats. This includes our basic human needs for food, shelter, clothing, warmth, and family relationships.

This instinct is highly focused on physical well-being,

safety, material safety, and everyday comfort. Every time our basic needs are threatened by the environment, we can use resource and energy hoarding to preserve what we have as a result of the external threat. We may consider this as the basic primal instinct possessed by all creatures. The drive for survival and self-preservation.

Social Instinct:

This social instinct is also called "the adaptive" instinct.

It's the need to get along with others and form secure social bonds. It's about creating a sense of belonging around you.

Today we see this a lot on social media with memberships and communities emerging where like-minded people (who feel the need to belong) are gathering. It's about focusing energy on working for shared purposes or the greater good.

. . .

This instinct is very much about being part of something that resonates with you where you feel secure, heard and valued within that group and community.

Sexual Instinct:

Sexual Instinct is also called "attraction" instinct.

It's the universal need to procreate and pass on our genes to continue. It governs our sexuality, intimacy, and the close friendships we cherish.

This instinct also directs the vitality of the life force within our bodies. It focuses on the intensity and passion contained in experiences and one on one relationship that leads us to search for opportunities that promise strong alliances, synergy, and deep connections.

This instinct is often confined to just sexual intimacy, but it's meant to be so much more. It's definitely about projecting yourself into the environment and experiencing intimate relationships that are pleasurable and extending your DNA, but it can also be about passing on ideas that help you create a legacy that goes far beyond your physical reach.

When we overlay these three human behaviour instincts with everything we've talked about so far, the end result is a combination of twelve. The set of combinations that falls into our most dominant type of personality helps us to connect with the intricacies of our daily behaviour and preferences.

"These instincts relate to the fundamental instinctual intelligence that develops within each of us to ensure our survival as individuals and as a human species.

Recent advances in neuroscience research have confirmed the strong and often invisible intelligence.

Self-Preservation Instinct	Social Instinct	Sexual Instinct
The need to preserve our body and its life force. Keeping away from threats. This includes our basic human needs of food, shelter, clothing, warmth and family relations.	The need to get along with others and form secure social bonds. It's about creating a sense of belonging around you.	The universal need to procreate and continue the human race generation after generation. It governs our sexuality, intimacy and the close friendships that we transmit as well as our legacy.
Type 1: The Perfectionist /Reformer	Type 1: The Perfectionist /Reformer	Type 1: The Perfectionist /Reformer
• Anxiety	• Non-adaptability	• Zealousness or Jealousy
Type 2: The Giver/Helper	Type 2: The Giver/Helper	Type 2: The Giver/Helper
• Privilege	• Ambition	• Seduction or Aggression
Type 3: The Achiever/Performer	Type 3: The Achiever/Performer	Type 3: The Achiever/Performer
• Security	• Prestige	• Charisma
Type 4: The Romantic/Individualist	Type 4: The Romantic/Individualist	Type 4: The Romantic/Individualist
• Fearlessness	• Shame	• Competition
Type 5: The Observer/Investigator	Type 5: The Observer/Investigator	Type 5: The Observer/Investigator
• Castle	• Symbols	• Confident
Type 6: The Loyalist/Doubter	Type 6: The Loyalist/Doubter	Type 6: The Loyalist/Doubter
• Warmth	• Duty	• Warrior
Type 7: The Enthusiast/Dreamer	Type 7: The Enthusiast/Dreamer	Type 7: The Enthusiast/Dreamer
• Networking	• Sacrifice	• Fascination
Type 8: The Challenger/Leader	Type 8: The Challenger/Leader	Type 8: The Challenger/Leader
• Survival	• Camaraderie	• Possessiveness
Type 9: The Peacemaker/Diplomat	Type 9: The Peacemaker/Diplomat	Type 9: The Peacemaker/Diplomat
• Strong Appetite	• Participation	• Fusion

Personality Type One: The Perfectionist also called the Reformer

Self-preservation Instinct:

The basic character drive here will be projected as anxiety.

This is the perfectionist who is constantly concerned and seeking to control everything. Their anxiety causes them to constantly try to anticipate risks, and they like to be prepared for it all. For them, attention to detail is likely an understatement. Usually they are very hard on themselves and take things rather seriously.

This subtype prefers to avoid expressing anger even if they feel it, and when interrupted they will often experience and show great frustration. The type one subtype has a very loud inner critic and tends to amplify their anxiety and worry.

Social Instinct:

The basic character drive here will be projected as Non-adaptability.

Fairness and making things right motivates this subtype. They are systematic thinkers, set high standards for themselves and others, and like being an example of integrity and principled conduct.

They practice a lot of self-control and can be quite friendly while in their own comfort zone. Because they are so linear and see everything in black and white, it can be hard to adapt to a new environment or situation, right or wrong. They can also become very resentful and critical with those who don't fit their right idea.

Sexual Instinct:

The basic character drive here will be projected as zealousness and/or jealousy.

This subtype will be highly charged, passionate and maintain high self-control standards. They have an idealistic view of how things should be and tend to want to reform others and fit them into "what's right."

Rage and anger will be expressed directly by those who fall into this subtype, especially if their efforts to improve others are restricted. They also prioritize their partner's attention and are usually very jealous of their partner or other people who seem to do better.

2. Personality Type Two: The Giver also called the Helper

Self-preservation Instinct:

The basic character drive here will be projected as Privilege.

This type two feels privileged and unique in some way because it invests heavily in creating warm nurturing relationships. They spend a lot of time looking after others and supporting them. As such, there's a tendency to become self-titled and even develop a prideful attitude that requires special privileges and approval as a result of care.

They are "nice" with a highly activated childlike spirit. This type two likes to be looked after but is not too keen on long-term commitments. Fear of rejection is a great deal for this subtype, and they can experience a great deal of hurt and abandonment when their needs are not met.

Social Instinct:

The basic character drive here will be projected as Ambition.

Forming the right alliances and having great allies is essential for this subtype because they want to build their self-esteem through visible achievements and social achievements. They enjoy taking on leadership roles and standing out from the crowd. They enjoy "being on" and build their influence based on the connections they form as well as their skills.

Those in this subtype do not actively demonstrate a child-like spirit (at least not as much as the other type twos) and tend to have a strategy of giving more than they get. Seeking recognition through ambition is more pronounced in this type of two personalities.

Sexual instinct:

The basic character drive here will be projected as Seduction and/or aggression.

This type two will focus all their energies, abilities and seductive abilities in forming and nurturing powerful and intimate relationships.

This type of person is passionate, resilient, strong-willed and willing. They are very devoted in their personal relationships, and they don't like taking no for an answer.

This type two uses seduction, which can go as far as turning into aggression if pushed into it, to gain the desired attention and recognition.

Although they like to use body language and feeling tones that can be found as seductive, it doesn't necessarily imply sexual desire.

3. The Achiever also called the Performer

Self-preservation Instinct:

The basic character drive here will be projected as Security.

This type three variation is highly focused on accomplishment and creating material success for itself. This type of person avoids being viewed as image-oriented and doesn't openly like to advertise their strengths. But it's still very important to them to be successful and to get recognition for their hard work. Financial success and the creation of a sense of security around them is an enormous priority for this subtype.

They work very hard and like to maintain high standards and a good image of success. This subtype three has an abundance of energy and tends to accomplish a lot.

The real danger for them is that they often lose contact with their authentic self in pursuing all that success and are prone to creating false identities and valuing themselves on the basis of their job role or social status.

Social Instinct:

The basic character drive here will be projected as Pr.

This type three variation is more interested in validating and receiving lots of social endorsement. They crave power, work hard to "know the right people" and focus a lot on gaining powerful leadership positions in government or business.

Prestige, praise, and influence are what this subtype will be after most, and they will generally train themselves to adjust to teams or organizations ' social norms and requirements if it helps them gain influence and power. They are highly competitive and love to be at the center of attention.

This particular subtype will have no problems promoting their ideas and achievements with confidence. Unlike the first type three who prefer not to advertise their achievements and success, this subtype would actually go to the extreme to make known theirs. And to cover up anything that doesn't align with that "perfect image of success."

Sexual Instinct:

The basic character drive here will be projected as Charisma.

Personal power and gender identification as well as all the issues that arise from that mostly drive three variations of this type. They have a lot to do with masculinity and femininity. Having a "movie star" life that means having the perfect outer image is what rocks your world. They are also very enthusiastic and charismatic, making them very likable.

It's very important to be attractive to others as a man or woman. But they also enjoy supporting others in their success and often have that enthusiastic attitude "if you succeed, I succeed."

The biggest challenge for this subtype, despite remaining very competitive, charismatic and powerful on the outside, is that those who fall into their subtype's unhealthy path often quietly struggle with confusing feelings about their sexuality. Tackling such conflicts can be tough as there's so much effort to appear as a powerful performer.

4. The Romantic also called the Individualist.

Self-preservation Instinct:

The basic character drive here will be projected as Fearlessness.

This type four variation will express their emotions less while still being very sensitive and idealistic. In a sense, we could say that the three subtypes are the least dramatic. But that doesn't mean they don't experience those tumultuous emotions, they just want to be seen as someone who doesn't complain.

The truth is that this type of person has just trained themselves to live with pain and suffering. They know how to internalize negative emotions and prefer being tough enough to deal with anything that comes along. Compared to the other subtypes, it makes them less likely to open up and share their feelings with others, but this doesn't mean that they lack empathy. In fact, they are trying very hard to reach out to and support those who are suffering around them.

This subtype is very creative and profoundly anxious to experience an authentic life, even though that sometimes means being a little reckless. They will have no trouble packing up and moving into a completely new environment if their self-preservation trigger makes them feel like an authentic experience is elsewhere.

The biggest challenge for this variation of personality type is the tension often created between the desire to build material security in their lives while remaining completely detached from it all. In fact, a person in this subtype finds comfort in suffering and expressing it to others. This tends to generate attention, support and sometimes admiration from others.

They often feel inadequate about social situations and easily become envious of the social status of other people or when they meet those who seem to have already found a place where they "belong." A sense of belonging really drives them and they strive to establish an acceptable social role where they can be heavenly. Their biggest issue is being able to overcome the social shame they often experience, and there's always a hidden inner conflict going on because they constantly doubt themselves and struggle with feelings of inferiority. A person in this subtype will notice a tendency to blame others, compare himself with others, and constantly struggle with deep shame and envy.

Sexual Instinct:

The basic character drive will be competition.

If the previous subtype can be called shameful, then this personality variation can be called' shameless.'

This subtype is very loud and vocal about ha. With a lot of vigour, they express their emotions and desires. It's what I call the queen or king of the classic drama. They are highly demanding and highly competitive. Because they believe in evaluating themselves on the basis of how they match other people, competition is a major motivation for this subtype, and they will do anything to beat the competition.

Unfortunately, this competitiveness comes from a place of deep-seated insecurity and inadequacy feelings. For this subtype, personal blocks and issues are always resurfacing as their sense of value and value is directly linked to beating those they consider strong and powerful.

5. The Observer also called the Investigator.

Self-preservation Instinct:

The basic character drive here will be projected in the form of The Castle.

This variation in personality is driven by the need to be very protective of the place they call home. Their personal space and privacy are far beyond limits, and they have no difficulty in setting clear boundaries for all. They enjoy living a comfortable and relatively lonely life with a few close friends.

A person in this subtype would prefer to sit back and watch social life rather than participate actively in it. They are very guarded and independent in choosing to cut off intimacy so as not to lower their guard and lose that sense of privacy and security.

Having a safe haven where they can retreat and take refuge from the world is essential for this subtype. And because they also like seclusion, having enough supplies is always a concern for them, which often leads to a minimalist lifestyle being hoarded and lived.

However, some subtypes go to the other extreme and choose to make their' castle' wherever they are and end up traveling forever or moving from place to place. They tend to be introverts, but not all, and prefer not to reveal much of their inner world.

Social Instinct:

The basic character drive here will be projected in the form of symbols.

This variation of personality type is brilliant and hungry for more knowledge. Their main focus is on searching for meaning and answers to the most important life issues. They take little to no pleasure in dealing with trivia every day. Their hunger for mastery and understanding of sacred symbols and language leads them down paths that are rarely traversed by ordinary human beings.

This subtype loves to connect and engage with other brilliant minds and experts who share their ideas and hunger for higher knowledge and knowledge. Unfortunately, they often get too stuck in too much critical thinking, analysis and interpretation that causes a snag in their ability to participate actively with others.

A person in this subtype tends to be very private, reclusive and quiet, unwilling to share their personal space or inner resources, but at the same time, when triggered to talk about a topic they're passionate about, they'll be the same. It's almost as if they can go from being completely introverted to being energetically extroverted by pushing a button.

Sexual Instinct:

The basic character drive here is projected in the form of The Confidant.

This type five variation is the most person-related and connected. They love keeping things confidential too, but with this slight change. A subtype five confidant in a private one-on - one relationship will open up and share intimate information about their inner world and frame of mind. But only to a selected few who undergo a series of loyalty tests for the first time.

This subtype possesses the cooler and analytical character traits and although still super secretive and reserved, once they find that "shared chemistry" with another they open up and enjoy the trust and connection that such a relationship allows.

The main challenge this subtype struggles with is the creativity of tension. The Doubter also called the loyalist.

Instinct for self-preservation:

The basic character drive here will be projected as warmth.

This type six variation is very affectionate and warm-hearted. But they are very pronounced in fear, anxiety, and insecurity. They try to overcome it by building strong relationships and bonds that will help them feel safe.

You will often find that an earlier childhood event may have created a lot of suppressed hurt that causes them to be very afraid of taking risks or making mistakes. As a result, this subtype will prefer to repress their negative emotions, particularly because they see it as a better and more cautious way to deal with such feelings, especially if they believe it could jeopardize the warmth of a relationship they really need.

A person in this subtype doesn't like feeling "left out" and is struggling to share their opinions openly. They prefers to stay within well-established boundaries and risk-taking is not easy.

Social Instinct:

The basic character drive here will be projected as A Sense of Duty.

This type six variation of personality is very focused

and concerned about living up to one's own duty. To those who belong to this subtype, integrity, fairness, and responsibility matter a lot. They believe in standing up for "the little guy" and defending the weak.

This subtype is highly rational and dedicated to their work, choosing to follow the rules and procedures set in their environment. They tend to be more black and white, connect with social ideals and enjoy working towards a greater cause.

A person in this subtype is very concerned about knowing the rules and making sure that everyone understands their role too often creating clear agreements with colleagues and friends to avoid confusion or unnecessary squabbling. The big challenge is the fear of rejection often brewing underneath and the deep sense of responsibility carried by their own duty which can either become a calling or a burden to them depending on how they develop their personality.

Sexual Instinct:

The basic character drive here will be projected as The Warrior.

This particular variation of personality type has two

styles. The first style is based on overcoming the undercurrent of fear through physical strength and bravery's willpower and feats. It can also be seen in gaining intellectual power.

By creating beauty in their environment, the second style is seen. Channelling their idealism and keen perceptiveness into creating beauty in the hopes that it will help them feel more in control and stable.

Both styles within this subtype indicate a bold assertiveness that often leads to bullying. A person in this subtype will undoubtedly experience a lot of self-doubt, fear, and instability and will often try to avoid it or overcome it by either running straight to it through a focus on strength or beauty. This need for security and power often clouds their ability to connect with their own emotions and leads to a lot of vulnerability struggle.

7. The Dreamer also called the Enthusiast.

Self-preservation Instinct:

The fundamental character drive here will be projected in the form of networking.

This variation of personality type loves to have good things in life and is surrounded by rich relationships, beauty, fun conversations and entertainment.

They love planning fun projects or events, preparing elaborate meals, dinin. Despite being more interested in family and friends, their energetic and enthusiastic approach to life and people makes them great in nurturing a "family" relationship that extends far beyond blood relatives. What motivates them is to ensure that everyone does well and has the best experience with them.

A person in this subtype is usually very good at getting what they want and justifying or defending what they want to do. The biggest challenge is the tendency to overdo things, become too self-interested or overindulge in some way with food, talk, shopping or stimulants.

Social Instinct:

The basic character drive here will be projected as Sacrifice.

This subtype tends to act against the common feature of insatiability shown by the other seven. They are generous and have a strong desire to make meaning in the world and make a difference. They are pleased to sacrifice their own needs in order to serve the needs of the group, family, organization or person they support. They have a utopian outlook on life, which usually serves them well.

However, an underlying current of dependence is experienced with this subtype because they need friends and other people or group-based projects to express themselves and feel they are doing something meaningful. They secretly hope to be recognized and appreciated for the sacrifices they make in all their self-sacrificing nature.

A person in this subtype is very generous, visionary in their thinking, focuses more on others, and is attracted to anything that seeks to fulfill a greater cause. Their primary challenge is the tendency to be highly judgmental of others and of themselves whenever they perceive a sense of selfishness appearing.

Sexual Instinct:

The basic character drive here will be projected as Fascination.

Here we find the classical dreamer and idealist. This variant of personality type sees the world by means of rose-colored filters. They's immediately attracted to new ideas, new people and potential adventure falling into a state of fascination immediately. But this suggestibility works both ways.

Not only is this subtype easily fascinated, but it fascinates others as well. Their charm can be very persuasive and irresistible, making such people great when it comes to sales and customer service.

A person in this subtype sees the good in everything and is always excited and optimistic. They're always connected to the stream of infinite possibilities.

The main challenge is to deal with things They sees as dull, dreary, boring and predictable. Conditions, individuals and even a dull world are completely unacceptable and become a source of frustration.

8. The Challenger also called the Leader.

Self-preservation Instinct:

The basic drive of character here will be projected as Survival.

This variation of personality will be more driven and focused on survival and protecting those under their care. More interested in ensuring success and security in physical and materials. These subtype eights are aggressive and excessive in their tendencies.

A typical mind attitude is "win or die fighting." Usually, this subtype is seen as a very powerful, productive and direct personality that never supports situations simply because things get tough. They are also very fiercely protecting their family and friends and are often perceived as the strong pillar that holds things together.

A person in this subtype is confident, secure, powerful, direct and will usually assume the role of guardian, father or mother. They're very concerned about protecting themselves, their surroundings, and those under their care. Survival is a major concern at all times.

Social Instinct:

The basic character drive here will be projected as a camaraderie.

This personality variation of eight still has the same type eight aggression and excessiveness, but it can be channelled differently. A sense of injustice and powerlessness is active among the individuals who fall into this subtype, which they try to resolve by forming groups or alliances to which they are very dedicated.

They focus more on social causes and prefer to be the group or alliance leader, serving the people for a higher mission. Unfairness, injustice or abuse of power triggers their sensitivities and they feel the need to protect against such things those under their influence. They prefer to support others rather than assert their own personal needs.

A person in this subtype will usually choose to mediate their anger by harnessing that energy to serve the needs of the members of the community they serve. They will also want to be the "shield" loyally protecting his or her tribe from unjust authority or any other type of danger.

Sexual instinct:

The fundamental character drive here will be projected as possessiveness.

This type eight variation demands control over others and loves to possess whatever they desire. They like being rebellious and have no fear of breaking the rules. Impulsive rules for this subtype, and very intense people are usually always ready to disrupt things and bring about change. They will never shy away from challenging the status quo and will need to drive change, gain power and influence over others.

When it comes to intimacy, the eight aggressions and possessively are still very pronounced, often wanting to dominate the partner entirely.

A person in this subtype will have the same aggressive and excessive qualities as all types eight, but with one distinct qualities. They're going to tend to take it a little too far.

There's a hunger for possession that can sometimes be good if it's aimed at serving a worthy cause. But if it's directed to something detrimental for them and others, it can also be dangerous. Sometimes this subtype of personality may be willing to let go and surrender if They feels a strong enough desire from a partner able to fully meet their needs.

9. The Peacemaker also called the Diplomat.

Self-preservation Instinct:

The basic character drive here will be projected as a Strong Appetite.

This personality variation is somewhat similar to an eight subtype in that they are very self-focused and concerned about meeting physical needs.

Material safety and the provision of daily comfort is very important. Those who fall into this subtype have a great appetite for food and possessing things.

A person is often a collector in this subtype. Very focused on meeting their personal needs and providing comfort to the material. They loves time alone and can become very irritable when someone threatens their sense of equilibrium or disrupts the daily rhythms that support their instinctual life. Material abundance is often more important than personal or spiritual growth.

Social Instinct:

The basic drive will be projected as a Powerful Need for Participation.

This variation in personality of the nine is the most friendly, selfless and warm type. Those who are in this subtype are usually strong, reliable, always in harmony with others and do a great job blending in with their friends ' agenda or the different social groups they become part of.

This subtype, often showing excellent leadership skills and selfless contribution, will position itself as the mediator or facilitator that comes naturally to them. Their instinctual motive is to be part of a wider group or the community benefactor. They don't like to burden others with their personal struggles so they usually maintain a happy attitude and focus on other people's needs and roles.

A person in this subtype is more interested in just feeling like they're participating in something meaningful. They's working hard to make those they love happy and willing to make whatever sacrifices are necessary to meet the needs of those under their care.

They are affectionate and friendly to do their utmost to be a reliable, concrete pillar for those in their care, even if it means neglecting their own pain and struggles.

Sexual Instinct:

The fundamental character drives here wil Union with others is their instinctual motive, and that can be either sexual or spiritual with another person, nature, or lifeitself.

This deep longing may sometimes be chaotic, or it may be the gateway to a transcendental experience. When partnered with others, they tend to feel more comfortable and secure and usually can not stand alone. As a result, there may be a tendency to go along with other people's demands and exclude their personal preferences.

A person in this subtype is usually very warm and affectionate with a deep urge for fusion. Their most important challenge is to make this practical in day-to-day living and keeping personal boundaries as well as focusing on oneself.

How to know your Subtype:

Before moving on to the next section, here are a few tips on how to recognize your subtype. This could be easy for some people. You could take the Enneagram test in a matter of minutes and figure out your center and subtypes. I'm happy if that's you. You're fine to go. Simply apply everything you've learned as you move forward in life.

However, if you're not that lucky and still feel lost, confused or even unable to figure out your subtype instantly, I've covered you. You're not on your own. This is something that is happening to many people. It requires more study and exploration over time, so let the process evolve naturally.

I think we all identify with all three instinctual drives to some extent. So if you find that's just knowing that there's nothing wrong with you. After all, in each of us, they all exist. But what is the most important thing for you in general? This is the clarity you need.

The subtypes of the Enneagram are not meant to be an accurate science. Rather, they are meant to evoke a specific theme and make you aware of the various seasons in your life and the different motives that influence your choices. The Enneagram personality tool is a dynamic growth-oriented system and is meant to be a personal inventory that aims to identify your basic fears motivations and strengths so that through a specific trajectory you can facilitate your personal growth.

If you can start by confidently identifying your primary type and the main intelligence center (one of the triads), then you will be able to discover. As you determine what to identify with, avoid becoming too rigid about this.

Look at the diagram I share below. A visual representation of your subtypes should be given to you. You may choose to start first by identifying with the most attractive instinct center. For example: If you feel genuinely driven by social instinct and the need to belong or fight for a higher cause within a group, then you can focus on the-social instinct-and match your Enneagram type to the corresponding subtype.

Self Preservation Instinct	Social Instinct	Sexual Instinct
The need to preserve our body and its life force. Keeping away from threats. This includes our basic human needs of food, shelter, clothing, warmth and family relations.	The need to get along with others and form secure social bonds. It's about creating a sense of belonging around you.	The universal need to procreate and continue the human race generation after generation. It governs our sexuality, intimacy and the close friendships that we innquire as well as our legacy.
Type 1: The Perfectionist /Reformer	Type 1: The Perfectionist /Reformer	Type 1: The Perfectionist /Reformer
•Anxiety	•Non-adaptability	•Zealousness or Jealousy
Type 2: The Giver/Helper	Type 2: The Giver/Helper	Type 2: The Giver/Helper
•Privilege	•Ambition	•Seduction or Aggression
Type 3: The Achiever/Performer	Type 3: The Achiever/Performer	Type 3: The Achiever/Performer
•Security	•Prestige	•Charisma
Type 4: The Romantic/Individualist	Type 4: The Romantic/Individualist	Type 4: The Romantic/Individualist
•Fearlessness	•Shame	•Competition
Type 5: The Observer/Investigator	Type 5: The Observer/Investigator	Type 5: The Observer/Investigator
•Castle	•Symbols	•Confident
Type 6: The Loyalist/Doubter	Type 6: The Loyalist/Doubter	Type 6: The Loyalist/Doubter
•Warmth	•Duty	•Warrior
Type 7: The Enthusiast/Dreamer	Type 7: The Enthusiast/Dreamer	Type 7: The Enthusiast/Dreamer
•Networking	•Sacrifice	•Fascination
Type 8: The Challenger/Leader	Type 8: The Challenger/Leader	Type 8: The Challenger/Leader
•Survival	•Camaraderie	•Possessiveness
Type 9: The Peacemaker/Diplomat	Type 9: The Peacemaker/Diplomat	Type 9: The Peacemaker/Diplomat
•Strong Appetite	•Participation	•Fusion

If that doesn't seem to yield clear results, try a different approach. Within the subtypes that most resonate with you, you may choose to write down all the nine sets. You'll probably feel more attracted to one of the sets of nine terms than the other two. The one that attracts you most should be the instinctual title that best describes your long-run habits, concerns, and anxieties.

My friend Joanna was at first struggling to identify her subtype. She thought she was a type four Ennea-gram personality with her dominant subtype being the instinct of self-preservation. Her husband was not in agreement. This created some doubt in her, and before she finally felt comfortable with her chosen Enneagram type and subtype, it took a lot of studies and deep reflection. Maybe at first you'll need to do the same. Keep going and let the drawings below guide you into your truth.

SECTION IV: USING THE ENNEAGRAM TO ENRICH YOUR LIFE

20

INTEGRATING AN ANCIENT TOOL INTO A MODERN LIVING

*T*here's no denying that the model of the Enneagram is as simple as it is profoundly complex.

The layers on the Enneagram system as shown in the previous chapter are then dissected. Fortunately for you, it won't take you a decade.

In fact, all you need to get started on your self-discovery is to take a test to learn your type in the nine-point system and figure out your subtype, so you can be well on your way to profound revelations about your behaviour, your strengths and how to grow.

The more you understand why you're doing what you're doing, the easier it's going to be for you. At the very least, you'll have a fresh new lens to interact with and understand those you meet in your everyday life. That is the power of the Enneagram.

This system, passed on for generations from ancient times to modern times, can become a handy tool for your personal growth, conflict resolution, and even development of characters.

Are there areas in your life that you have been struggling with?

Do you have painful relationships because you just don't seem to be able to make them work the way you think they should work? Are there people in your workplace or you can't see eye to eye at home, yet you know that you just have to find a way to get along because of the commitments that you have made?

Is it your body that just doesn't seem to listen or respond positively to anything you're trying to do?

All these issues can be improved with the use of this tool.

ACCELERATING YOUR PERSONAL
GROWTH AND SELF-EXPRESSION

*P*ersonal growth and self-expression are as essential as breathing for us as human beings.

All these issues can be improved with the use of this tool. The desire for self-expression arises naturally once we secure the basic needs that help us to feel safe and comfortable. It's meant to be part of our evolution and self-realization.

Self-expression doesn't necessarily mean that art is produced, written, performed, or any of that. It may necessarily include that for some people, but at its core, it's about communicating your truth and using body language, your work and actions, and how you interact and engage in your world with others. This also includes how you dress, how you drive your car, how you decorate your home, etc.

The main challenge with personal growth and self-expression comes when there feels like there's a block or a lack of inspiration and creativity to get through something you want to portray to someone else in some way.

If you've ever been in a situation where you really wanted to express something that was weighing on your heart, but for whatever reason you've not been able to get this emotion out.

This is a common problem when we do not yet understand the motives, instincts and behaviours that affect our personalities. We may have an idea of what we want to communicate, but we are short on execution or full demonstration.

The other day I was watching a baking show, and one of the contestants competing to win $10,000 started crying when her cake looked like nothing she had imagined in her mind. Even the judges had a hard time scoring her because they could see her anguish and the fact that she couldn't manifest what-ever creative idea she had at the start of the competition.

The reason why personality tool Enneagram works so well to improve people's lives is because it helps them better understand their strengths, hang-ups, instinctual drives and warning signs to watch. This tool also highlights the underlying fears that often guide our behaviour.

Don Richard Riso and Russ Hudson reveal the nine core fears that everyone needs to be aware of in "The Wisdom of The Enneagram."

Type One: Fear of being evil or corrupt.

This type of personality strives to be morally upright and virtuous in the face of external corruption. They tend to be perfectionist, sweating even minute details at all times. And their underlying fear is corruption. So the drive for meticulousness and virtual action is driven by the need to prove that fear is wrong. Motivated by their own sense of integrity, individuals who are type one personality will constantly strive to move away from corruption to virtue.

Type Two: fear of being unloved or unwanted by others

This type of personality strives to be loved and desired by those around them. They give, nurture and invest a lot of their time, effort and resources to cultivate relationships in order to overcome the inherent fear of not being lovable. The giving and helping that comes from people in the type two personality comes from a place where they prove that they deserve to be cared for and loved by others because they give it too much. They will constantly strive to move away from worthlessness and towards relationships that foster mutual love and caregiving.

Type Three: fear of being worthless and unfulfilled

This type of personality aims to achieve success and status quo as the right measure of their own worth. The underlying fear here is a sense of worthlessness inherent in it. This type feels that they are not desirable apart from their accomplishments and must therefore accomplish as much as possible to be desired and accepted by others. They will strive to move continuously from worthlessness to impressive achievements that can earn great admiration and respect.

Type Four: fear of lacking a unique, special and significant identity.

With this type of personality comes the need to prove to others their uniqueness and individuality. The underlying fear in personality type four is that They would be unworthy and unlovable if they were "ordinary" or "average." As such, they seek to create a unique identity to prove their meaning in the world.

Those who are a personality type four are constantly moving from normal to expressions of individuality and intensity. They are afraid to be helpless, overwhelmed and unable to deal with the world around them. As a result, they try to learn as much as they can and master as much as they can to feel safe, skilled and able to handle the world. Those in this type of personality are constantly striving to move away from ignorance and ambiguity towards knowledge and understanding.

Type Six: Fear of being without support or guidance.

This type six personality is striving to find guidance and support from those around them. Their underlying fear is that they themselves are unable to survive. As such, they always seek as much other people's support and direction as possible. Those who fall into this type of personality are constantly striving to move away from isolation and towards other people's structure, security, and guidance.

Type Seven: Fear of deprivation and pain

This type seven personality strives to achieve their

wildest desires and find satisfaction. Their underlying concern is that their needs and desires will not be met by others. Rather, they feel they have to go and pursue on their own what they want. Those in this type of personality strive to move away from pain, sadness, and helplessness toward independence, happiness, and fulfilment.

Type 8: fear of being harmed or controlled by others

This type of personality strives to be independent, powerful, influential, and self-directed. Their underlying concern is to be betrayed, controlled, or otherwise violated. This type of personality can not be controlled or at the mercy of others. Only when they are in control of their circumstances do they feel safe and fine. Those who fall into this type of personality are constantly moving away from outside limitations to self-sufficiency and power.

Type Nine: fear of loss and separation from others.

This type of personality strives to maintain harmony and peace both internally and externally. Their underlying fear is that they will be separated from others and disconnected. They're afraid the world around them will go out of sync. As such, they will do all they can to live in harmony with other people and the world around them because this creates a sense of security and connectivity. Those in this type of personality usually strive to move away from conflict and pain and toward stability, peace, and harmony.

By understanding your primary type of Enneagram, your basic fears, and your subtype, your natural gifts are fully appreciated, and limitations are not so mysterious.

It becomes easier to find satisfaction in your work and relationships. You'll better equipped to handle situations, hostile environments, and impulsive behaviours. For instance, if you have a deep longing for others to feel positively about you, you might have problems knowing when to say "no" to something because you're predisposed to wanted to please people. So maybe if you're asked to do double shifts at work, you might say, "yes," even if it hurts you. In such a situation, learning to say "no" would be the healthier, more satisfying answer, yet you would only have this awareness of yourself if you really understood more about your personality type.

Some people can quickly spot their primary and subtype personalities while it takes time, study and constant self-reflection for others. I don't know how long it's going to take you, but I encourage you to start because the sooner you do, the faster you're going to be able to create a healthier, more balanced life. Before moving on to the impact and benefit of using this tool and the insights gained to improve your relationships, I invite you to take the Enneagram test and discover your primary type as well as your wings, center and subtype.

22

ENNEAGRAM TEST

*L*et's take a quick look at the main personality types before you jump into our interactive online test:

Type 1: Reformer

If this is you, then you're not once to hesitate. You're purpose driven, set high standards for yourself, and are very self-controlled.

Type Two: Helper

If this is your primary type, then you're driven by the need for others to be loved and cared for. You're generous, compassionate, humble, and uplifting. There's a deep desire to feel loved and accepted, and sometimes the gift can be made in an effort to secure that state of love.

Type Three: Attain

If this is your primary type, then you're more focused on being the best. You want others to perceive you as being successful. You're usually very assertive, winning is all, and it matters a lot to your personal image.

Type Four: Romantic

If this is your primary type, then you have an impeccable eye for beauty in everything you do. You're more attuned to your and others ' emotions and can be quite dramatic at times. You're a romantic at heart, and a sanctuary to be treasured is your inner fantasy world.

Type Five: Observer

If this is your primary type, concentrate on knowledge and gain more knowledge. With a deep hunger for new ideas and greater understanding, you're highly intellectual. You can articulate new paradigms in a visionary way, and although you prefer isolation, when you're invited to speak on a topic, you can be very welcoming and engaged.

Type six: Loyalist

If this is your core personality type, then you're full

of courage. You're self-confident and trustworthy. You often struggle with self-doubt and doubt others, which can create a rollercoaster of emotions for you, but you're very committed and decisive when you're not in doubt.

Type 7: Enthusiast

If this is your primary type, then fun and spontaneity is your thing. Being around you is fun, playful and pleasant. You have a very positive outlook and savour the world's wealth. However, you tend to get distracted easily, and you always seem to be moving to the next exciting adventure, but if you're not scattered around or distracted, you have the potential for tremendous accomplishments.

Type 8: Challenger

If this is your primary type, then you're intense! You like to be with others directly. You're concerned about productivity, high energy and excellence in your work. You're self-determined, generous, and you have a big heart. Others generally perceive you as very powerful, which can sometimes make you seem somewhat intimidating and controlling, especially when you try to gain control and influence over others.

Type nine: Peacemaker

Peace and harmony are your primary driver if you fall into a type nine personality. You're authentic, unpretentious, and patient, you get along with everybody, you love serving others, and you put your needs first. At your best, you can recognize, encourage and help bring out the best in others.

Take the test now and once you have your results to go back to section II to read a more in-depth description of your type, then jump into section III to find out what kind of layered cake you have.

To access the test, simply copy and paste the following link into your browser:

https://bit.ly/2xEWljI

Remember what we said about the subtypes being like layers of a cake that we all have?

It means that you already have all three basic instincts, but one is going to be more dominant. By discovering how your cake is layered, you will begin to be more awake in your daily choices, and some of your impulses, reactions, and experiences will make more sense.

You're a type of personality combined with your

wings and center as well as your layered basic instincts now give you a detailed understanding of what makes you tick. And what a release that becomes as you step into improving your relationships with others.

23

CULTIVATING HEALTHY LOVING RELATIONSHIPS

*C*ultivating healthy, nourishing relationships is vital to us all. But we know how tough it can be with constant demands, especially in our modern society. That's why choosing your relationships wisely is even more critical than ever before.

The people you associate with and invest your energy both personally and professionally impact your well-being and success directly. That's why I encourage you to get better with the right people around you. But who is the right person?

In particular, when introducing Enneagram type combinations, a critical point to remember here is that no paring is particularly blessed or doomed to work out. The mistake so many people make is to avoid or undervalue all the other types once they learn about these Enneagram combinations. Focusing on a particular combination doesn't guarantee that you will be happy, nourished and in love.

What you want to achieve is another goal. You want to make sure the healthy versions of your types are displayed by both you and the person concerned. As long as two of you (regardless of type) are healthy, it will be amazing to experience together.

This is not always the norm, unfortunately. That's where it comes to play with self-discovery and further education. The better you're informed about the type, health level and tendencies of the other person, the greater your insight into the relationship. This is such a great tool to help you deepen your relationships as it will make you both aware of your behaviours. Once you shed light on your underlying fears, motives and natural tendencies as well as your gifts, you will have a choice as to how to respond to relationships in your life.

Regardless of your current needs for relationships, whether it's building healthy professional relationships with customers or cultivating a passionate, intimate relationship with your significant other. It will help you to love more in the present and to have a more grounded experience in your true nature.

Finally, when you act out of fear and when you act out of your own truth, you will be able to recognize. It will also enable you to discern the desires of your true self and those that are superficial.

It becomes easy to love and live in harmony with others once you have this level of clarity and self-awareness. Instead of reacting when things don't go the way you want in a relationship, you'll feel empowered to react with love, support, encourage, and bring out the best in others. You'll also become a better communicator, more importantly. And we all know how important communication is in a healthy relationship.

One of my best friends has recently experienced the power to use this Enneagram tool to help both her self-discovery and her fiancé.

There's no doubt in her mind how much Tom loves her. He's the most generous, warm, appreciative, careful, playful, and nurturing man she's ever met. They make the perfect couple because their personality seems to be complimented by him. She says, "I feel so loved and special when I'm with him. There's no one else I'd like to marry, but at times he can be somewhat controlling, needy and insincere, and it really created friction between us."

That was before I suggested that both of them study the Enneagram. She had already taken the test, so it wasn't too far-fetched an idea, but before Tom agreed it took a little bit of convincing. She told me her relationship had completely transformed in less than a month. She's found new ways to show her love and feels more compassion when some of her weaknesses appear.

They have increased their level of intimacy and communication. Above all, their behaviors are less like a mysterious enemy trying to sabotage one another's love. I can only assume that their self-discoveries will enrich their future marriage even more.

Although I will choose to focus more on personal and intimate relationships, the same concept can be applied to any relationship with which you wish to work.

Returning the magic of passionate love:

There's nothing more exciting than finding someone who "gets you." When you have discovered your type of Enneagram and use it to improve as well as enhance who you really are, it will change how you approach relationships forever.

This is not a reading of the horoscope, but a tool to use to determine the best type of people that will complement and enhance your whole life. I'm not saying it's an exact science, but when you learn about the personality types of your loved ones, you'll be amazed at how harmonious your relationships will be. The tendencies that usually hold you back from having healthy relationships with yourself and others won't be a mystery anymore. After all, the happier you become, the easier it will be to nurture healthy relationships.

Suggested combination types from the Enneagram Institute:

There are some insights into relationships for each type that could be a great starting point if you're looking for new loving relationships to manifest:

Type 1: The Perfectionist or Reformer
Best type combinations: 1 2 3 4 5 6 7 8 9

Type 2: The Giver or Helper
Best type combinations: 1 2 3 4 5 6 7 8 9

Type 3: The Achiever or Performer
Best type combinations: 1 2 3 4 5 6 7 8 9

Type 4: The Romantic or Individualist
Best type combinations: 1 2 5 4 6 6 7 8 9

Type 5: The Observer or Investigator
Best type combinations: 1 2 3 4 5 6 7 8 9

Type 6: The Loyalist or Doubter
Best type combinations: 1 2 3 4 5 6 7 8 9

Type 7: The Enthusiast or Dreamer
Best type combinations: 1 2 3 4 5 6 7 8 9

Type 8: The Challenger or Leader
Best type combinations: 1 2 3 4 5 6 7 8 9

Type 9: The Peacemaker or Diplomat
Best type combinations: 1 2 3 4 5 6 7 8 9

I know it's hard to hear, but if you kick your heels

back and relax once in a while, the world won't crumble. Release the need for constant monitoring of each outcome. It's also great to share your core values and motivations openly with your loved ones. Let them know how much you care and invite them into that vision to improve the world. Those who "get you" will be more than just encouraging your tendencies and supporting them.

Type Two: The Giver

Having discovered that you're warm, empathetic and motivated by the need to be loved and needed, this is your suggestion for a relationship.

Fight the urge to always jump in and fix the problems of other people, even if you're great at it. Learn to be there without getting too absorbed in their world for your significant other and often step out of the box to get in touch with your feelings. Ask yourself, "How am I doing?"

Type Three: The Achiever

Discovering that you're motivated by success, winning big, and being wired for high performance and productivity, here is your suggestion for a relationship.

You have a lot to offer, not just material success and

social status. Connect to the "more" you have. You're not always bound by someone's appreciation and value to your accomplishments. Learn how to make authentic connections and do not shy away from deep diving under the prestige and material success you have.

Type Four: The Romantic

Having discovered that you're a natural romantic with an eye for beauty and that you're more creative and expressive than most, here is your suggestion for a relationship.

Learn to take control of your emotions or they will control you and create constant problems. Without consuming you, you can become more aware of your emotions. Since you know, there's a tendency to be a queen or king of drama and that you're particularly sensitive when you feel misunderstood, communicate this to your loved one and help them know this side of you so that when it happens they too can respond accordingly. Use your power of perception to put yourself in the shoes of the one you love so that you can see things from their side of the table, then you will always know the right thing to do in any given situation.

Type Five: The Observer

Having discovered that you're the private, analytical type motivated by a hunger to gain more knowledge, here is your suggestion for a relationship. Just do it! Don't worry about being "pulled in" close by someone else where chemistry aligns. Your feelings are not too much to be dealt with by someone else, and you have what it takes to be good at this. Learn to reconnect more with your heart so that you can know when it's time to make the shift from head to heart.

Type Six: The Loyalist

Having discovered that you're the practical, committed, but always anxious type, here's your suggestion for your relationship.

Not everyone has a "hidden agenda." I know it's hard to hear and you're having a hard time being optimistic, but it's not going to make you feel optimistic. Your ability to be a great and loyal friend, always reliable and trustworthy, is a power that should not be underestimated in our modern world in particular. Learn how to use this power to build a robust and reliable bond with a significant other.

Type 7: The Enthusiast

With the new discovery of your type as fun, spontaneous and motivated by pleasure searching for experiences that stimulate you, here's your relationship advice.

Your positive, fun-loving attitude is contagious and will always attract great people to you, but you have to do it. Find the courage to face what might drive you to activities that are restless and shallow. It's not such a bad thing you know to be committed to the right person? You have so much greatness and wisdom to offer that you start to work on being more focused on body and mind.

Type 8: The Challenger

There's no doubt about it, you're fierce and intense. You're powerful, full of energy, strong and motivated by a need to control the underdogs and protect them. Here's a relationship tip that can help you cultivate amazing connections.

Vulnerability is not a bad thing in their eyes, especially with the one you love. Be all right to express any emotions that come up for you. The real you can be handled by people who love you. The real power you possess is the ability to show strength and tenderness when the situation demands it. Don't hold back or fight those rare moments as they become your most magical with the one you love.

Type Nine: The Peacemaker

Having discovered that you're the laid-back, harmonious guy who always gets along with everybody here is a piece of advice for you.

Yes, you're a peacemaker, but you don't always have to "settle" for something if you don't really want it. And being the wonderful mediator you're, even if they differ, it can be easier to express your needs and desires to someone else. Although it makes you uncomfortable, you have permission to voice a contrasting opinion to your significant other. The one who really loves you will appreciate your knowledge of the frame of mind and perspective of things even more. So go on, tell your truth!

24

MAPPING YOUR MOST JOYFUL AND
FULFILLING PATH

a s we said at the beginning of our journey in self-discovery and understanding of the Enneagram, this typing system is based on an ancient practice developed over the years to help us apply it better.

The modern Enneagram as we know it's divided into a nine-point system and subdivided into three triads or centres. The triads represent the head, the heart, and the gut, alternatively referred to as the center of thought, the center of feeling, and the center of instincts, which form the essential components of the human psyche.

While there are so many personality-typing systems available today, the Enneagram stands out from the crowd and for this particular reason maintains its global merit. Not only does it plunge deeper into variations that you will experience even within your dominant type, it also adds a unique aspect to things.

Namely:

You're given the direction of integration, which explains how your type is likely to behave on a health and growth pathway. And you're also given the direction of disintegration, which describes how your type is likely to act under pressure and stress.

This means that your self-discovery goes much deeper than the usual personality typing systems because it gives you the power to introspect and make new conscious choices in any area of your life, including relationships. For anyone interested in taking their personal growth and self-awareness to the next level, it's a vital tool.

The Enneagram is a tool designed to help you observe your personality (ego) and how it works closer. Being aware of who you really are, the basic instincts that drive your behavior and the quality of character that you can build to create either a healthy progressive path in life or a disintegrative path is the beginning of your self-discovery.

Depending on your core personality type, there are

some passions to become vigilant and work towards transformation at a fundamental level. The more you reflect on your behaviors and motives, the easier it will be to turn them into healthy virtues because, as you recall at the beginning of the book, we affirmed that each of us is pure and good in essence.

Here is a quick recap of the passions or behaviors that may unconsciously govern your life, plus how to transform them into healthy virtues. By taking the online test to which we provided the link in a previous chapter, the best way to figure out your type is. By answering all the questions honestly, your top score will show you what type of personality you are. Bear in mind, you might have multiple high scores because, as we said, the Enneagram is a complex, interconnected system just as a human being is complex and therefore can not be rigidly restricted to just one strict type.

Alternatively, you could go back to the earlier chapters and read through all the detailed descriptions of all personality types and try to decide which one is yours. If you feel that you know yourself well enough to identify your type instantly, then you can continue to study and understand your chosen type and all the additional information that we have shared in this book.

How the Enneagram can help you grow and manifest a joy-filled life.

The Enneagram is like a roadmap that empowers your self-observation capability and shows you how to reach higher levels of consciousness. The more you develop a clear vision of the healthiest and best version you can be, the more your life will be joyful and prosperous. It can be as simple as you want it to be, or as complex. Beginning with the basics is recommended. This book covers all the basics and some in-depth understanding of the system's intricacies. That doesn't mean that our studies end there, though. You can still dive deeper into your self-determined core personality type, wings and subtype by venturing into what is referred to as developmental levels.

In 1977, Don Riso discovered and began developing what is now known as the nine developmental levels which are the internal structures that make up the personality type itself. In other words, what Don Riso teaches is that you have an internal structure that is the core of your personality. There are layers within these internal structures and a certain behavioral demonstration of your personality type will be pronounced depending on your level. The range extends from healthy, average, and down to lower, unhealthy levels.

Don Riso and Russ Hudson further enhanced this discovery in the 1990s. They are the only Enneagram teachers in their Enneagram teachings to include this internal structure. The book recommended in chapter nine "The Enneagram's Wisdom" can also help you better understand what these teachers mean by levels of development plus how to rise higher in your development.

They have developed these nine levels of development to provide a "skeletal" structure of each type that can be very useful for therapists, counselors and other medical professions working with a client. By learning more about the nine levels of development within their personality type and where they are at a given time along that continuum, you can understand whether the person works within the healthy, average or unhealthy range and support them accordingly. Don Riso has other books available online, but I specifically encourage you to check out the The Wisdom of The Enneagram if you feel ready to dive into more details about your core personality. With the information shared in this book alone, you can quickly improve your work, health relationships and overall lifestyle.

So if you don't want to be an expert on this, don't worry. You already have all the knowledge you need to enhance your self-reflection and awareness ability. Naturally, the rest will unfold as you continue to work on understanding yourself and improving the areas of weakness that come to your conscious awareness.

Now that you have made the first few steps forward, there's no return. You can never be the same again for your work, relationships and how you perceive yourself. You will have a better chance of controlling yourself in whatever environment or situation you end up in if you have done the inner work. Planning for your future goals will also have more confidence. Having this inner and outer equilibrium is what you need in our modern world to thrive as your true self. Now that you're better at understanding and getting the tool out and cultivating the quality of life you've always wanted!